CW00550982

Advance Praise for

Timber Framing for the Rest of

With more than thirty years of hands-on experience, Rob Roy brings
solid insight and understanding of the importance of timber framing to all
aspects of natural building. This eminently readable, beautifully illustrated
book offers both practical advice and personal experience.

— ROBYN GRIGGS LAWRENCE, Editor-in-Chief, *Natural Home* magazine

If you want to build a home or barn without spending a fortune, you should
read this book. Modern timber framing techniques are easy to learn and perfect for
building with straw bales, cordwood masonry, cob, structural insulated panels
(SIPs) or local timber. The chapter about low-cost chainsaw mills for
cutting your own lumber, alone, is worth the price of the book.

— CHERYL LONG, Editor-in-Chief, *Mother Earth News*

In *Timber Framing for the Rest of Us,* Rob continues his good work of stocking
the shelves of the owner-builder's library. His books provide accessible information
and inspiration to a new generation of hands-on homeowners.

— MARK KLEIN, Gimme Shelter Construction, Amherst, WI

This is a wonderful reference for anyone considering timber frame construction,
and is somewhat intimidated by the exactness of the craft. Rob Roy has blended this
beautiful time-honored technique with state-of-the-art joinery components to
make timber framing available to all. However, there's more than just
nuts and bolts to this book, Rob also provides useful information on
frame design, structural load calculations, lumber procurement and more.
If you're looking for an alternative to conventional construction but aren't
quite ready to tackle a traditional timber frame this books for you.

— DON OSBY, builder and art director of *BackHome* Magazine

Rob Roy provides a wealth of basic information, tools and techniques for heavy
timber construction, employing "bolts and ingenuity." He offers a comprehensive and
comprehendible alternative to traditional timber framing for people with a wide range
of skills and experiences, all delivered in the lively and charming style we have
come to expect from his work in other areas.

— JOEL C. MCCARTY, Timber Framers Guild

Books for Wiser Living from Mother Earth News

Today, more than ever before, our society is seeking ways to live more conscientiously. To help bring you the very best inspiration and information about greener, more-sustainable lifestyles, New Society Publishers has joined forces with *Mother Earth News*. For more than 30 years, *Mother Earth* has been North America's "Original Guide to Living Wisely," creating books and magazines for people with a passion for self-reliance and a desire to live in harmony with nature. Across the countryside and in our cities, New Society Publishers and *Mother Earth News* are leading the way to a wiser, more sustainable world.

Timber Framing
for the Rest of Us

ROB ROY

NEW SOCIETY PUBLISHERS

Cataloguing in Publication Data

A catalog record for this publication is available from the National Library of Canada.

Copyright © 2004 by Rob Roy. All rights reserved. Second printing, November 2004.

Cover design by Diane McIntosh. Front cover images by David Fraser and Joe Zinni. Back cover images by Jim Juczak and Steve Chappell.
Interior design by Jeremy Drought.
Printed in Canada by Friesens Inc.

New Society Publishers acknowledges the support of the Government of Canada through the Book Publishing Industry Development Program (BPIDP) for our publishing activities.

Paperback ISBN: 0-86571-508-4

Inquiries regarding requests to reprint all or part of *Timber Framing for the Rest of Us* should be addressed to New Society Publishers at the address below.

To order directly from the publishers, please add $4.50 shipping to the price of the first copy, and $1.00 for each additional copy (plus GST in Canada). Send check or money order to:

New Society Publishers
P.O. Box 189, Gabriola Island, BC V0R 1X0, Canada
1 (800) 567•6772

New Society Publishers' mission is to publish books that contribute in fundamental ways to building an ecologically sustainable and just society, and to do so with the least possible impact on the environment, in a manner that models this vision. We are committed to doing this not just through education, but through action. We are acting on our commitment to the world's remaining ancient forests by phasing out our paper supply from ancient forests worldwide. This book is one step towards ending global deforestation and climate change. It is printed on acid-free paper that is **100% old growth forest-free** (100% post-consumer recycled), processed chlorine free, and printed with vegetable based, low VOC inks. For further information, or to browse our full list of books and purchase securely, visit our website at www.newsociety.com

NEW SOCIETY PUBLISHERS   www.newsociety.com

Dedication

To George Holden, Highland farmer, artist and friend.
Thanks for showing me that we can do most anything,
if we just put our minds to it.

Acknowledgments

A LOT OF PEOPLE OVER A LONG PERIOD OF TIME helped make this book possible. I would like to thank:

Geoff Huggins, Mark Powers, Joe Zinni, Larry Schuth, Jim Juczak, Richard Flatau, Chris Ryan, Jim Washburn, George Stuart, Ki Light, contractors Russell Pray and John Light, Steve Sugar and Eileen Hogan, and Terry at K Bay on Hawaii's Big Island for sharing their timber framing experiences.

Will Beemer of Heartwood Building School for timely materials and for introducing me to the Timber Framer's Guild.

Timber framer and author Steve Chappell for permission to use three illustrations from his book, *A Timber Framer's Workshop*, and for cheerfully answering questions.

Bob Samuelson for great advice on obtaining salvaged timbers.

Marie Cyburt Taluba for a drawing she did back in 1977 for my first book, a drawing used again here.

Doug Anderson of Winter Panel Corporation in Vermont for good information about stressed-skin and structural insulated panels.

Darin Roy, Rohan Roy, Anna Milburn-Lauer, Bruce Kilgore, Diane Lukaris, Stephanie Bayan, Doug Kerr, John Light, Peter Allen and Dawn Palmer for help with the new Earthwood sunroom, without which the important Chapter Five would not exist.

Richard R. Chapman at Simpson Strong-Tie Company, Inc.; Bette Gahres at Sterling Publishing Co., Inc.; and Margaret M. Leddin of the International Code Council for permissions to use copyrighted illustrations and tables.

Daniel Rimann, P.E., for reviewing Chapter Two on Timber Frame Structure and Appendix B on Stress Load Calculations. His corrections and suggestions were valuable, but any errors left behind are mine alone.

Bob Curnings at Prazi USA for supplying a picture of their Beam Cutter attachment for circular saws.

Long-time friend and *BackHome Magazine* editor Richard Freudenberger for his fine manuscript editing and permission to use the picture on page 57. (Isn't he a good-looking guy?) It's been great to finally work with Richard on a book-length manuscript.

The New Society gang is a pleasure to work with, even when crises occur. Thanks to:

Editor-in-Chief Chris Plant for his faith in the book.

Ingrid Witvoet for coordinating the text editing and Greg Green for his usual fine art editing.

Diane McIntosh for the cover design and Jeremy Drought for the interior layout.

Finally, and not least, loving thanks to my wife and building co-conspirator, Jaki, for her patience and her valuable help on photography, manuscript preparation, and with finding missing pictures. Now, as I write on February 16th, 2004, the galleys are proofed and this page is my last act on this book. Jaki will be getting at least some of her table surfaces back … until the next book (which begins next week.)

Rob Roy
Earthwood
West Chazy, New York

Contents

Introduction

*T*imber Framing for the Rest of Us. *Us* implies *Them*, or *They* or *Not Us*. And who are these others? They are no less than the skilled timber-framers, using time-tested methods of creating beautiful, strong, and enduring buildings throughout the world. At its best, timber framing done by traditional methods of joinery yields a quality of construction that spans the range from craft to art.

The use of timber-framing joinery, such as scarf, mortise-and-tenon, and rabbet joints, evolved during a time before metal fasteners were available, and its traditional use continued when metal spikes would have been expensive. Quality wood-on-wood timber framing continues to this day, and is a joy to see. There are plenty of good books to show how the work is done, and building schools that will teach the owner-builder these skills. Books are listed in the Bibliography, and schools and other resources are listed in Appendix C.

I have the highest admiration for these traditional builders. A good friend, who died much too young, took great pride in restoring historic timber frame buildings in Northern New York, often working to 1/64-inch (0.39 millimeter) tolerance. But the reality is that most timber framing is not done in the old-fashioned "traditional" way with wooden pegs, mortise-and-tenon joints, and the like. With the advent of relatively inexpensive mechanical fasteners, most builders — contractors and owner-builders alike — rely on other methods of joining, using things such as truss plates, screws and bolts, pole-barn nails, and even gravity. The problem is that there is a shortage of information about joining heavy timbers by these methods. Most construction manuals are quite good about describing the joining of "two-by" lumber — usually 1½ inches (3.81 centimeters) thick nowadays — and that's the extent of it. Chapter 1 speaks about traditional timber framing ... and the kind that this book is about.

However, many of the *natural building* methods which are becoming re-popularized today — such as cordwood masonry, straw bale construction, and cob building — benefit from heavy timber construction, primarily because these methods involve thick walls. There is also a great practical advantage in erecting a timber frame first, getting the roof on as a protective umbrella, and then infilling the structure using one or more of these natural — and typically slow — building methods. Before starting, though, it's good to have an understanding of the basic structural elements of timber framing, which is what Chapter 2 is all about. You'll also need the timbers themselves. Where to get them is the subject of Chapter 3.

Yes, you can accomplish all this with "traditional" wood-on-wood joining methods. I have even met two or three who have done so and my hat is off to them. But to do it right, a great deal of time and study must be expended, and there are a few specialized tools which need to be purchased. The reality is that most farmers, contractors, and owner-builders use methods of heavy timber framing which they have simply picked up from colleagues, relatives, or neighbors. And they use common tools found around the homestead, such as chainsaws, hammers, and electric drills. For years, I have felt that there has been a void in the literature for owner-builders on this subject, and that is why I have undertaken this volume as a kind of "missing link." Chapter 4 explains the basics of timber framing for the rest of us.

My qualifications are unpretentious. I've written about alternative building methods for almost thirty years and, with my wife Jaki, I've built four houses, a garage, and quite a few smaller outbuildings using the methods described herein. In fact, Jaki and I built a new addition to our Earthwood house in 2002, and the primary reason for it was to demonstrate and document some simple joining principles for this book. Chapter 5 takes you through this entire project from design to completion, step by logical step.

This book is not meant to document all of the methods and fasteners that are available. Rather, it demonstrates and describes the basic principles of building with heavy timbers by "non-traditional" methods (even though these non-traditional methods are certainly more common nowadays than the traditional ones.) It will show how to build very strong structures with a minimum of wood-joining skills.

Finally, to the expert timber framing craftsmen and teachers like Steve Chappell, Will Beemer, Jack Sobon, Tedd Benson, and so many others, I say that is not my intention to diminish your fine work in any way. Rather, I hope it will enhance appreciation of the craftsmanship that you practice and teach so generously, and, at the same time, offer a viable alternative. Those with time and inclination may want to incorporate some traditional joints in their project, especially where they can be left exposed. I have done this once or twice and was rather proud of myself afterwards.

In July of 2004, students at the author's Earthwood Building School in West Chazy, New York, built this octagonal timber frame in three afternoons, using the techniques described in **Timber Framing for the Rest of Us.** *The book sereved as the textbook for the morning classroom sessions. See page 154 for Earthwood Building School contact information, to learn about future workshops.*

CHAPTER ONE

About Timber Framing

A Little Background

THE BEGINNINGS OF QUALITY TIMBER FRAMING ARE LOST IN PRE-HISTORY, but a reasonable surmise is that simple frames could have been made by supporting beams on columns which had a natural fork at the top, the kind of thing that we boys of the 1950s saw in Boy Scout manuals or Straight Arrow cards stuffed as premiums in Shredded Wheat boxes. (Gee, I wish I still had those!) Once a horizontal timber is supported by the verticals, considerations such as stability and strength enter the equation. Early builders would have recognized the inherent strength of the triangle. The value of the pitched roof would have been recognized soon thereafter, and timber-frame structures were off and running. Refinements in both kind and degree would have evolved by trial and error, a kind of structural evolution, with failed tests being dropped by the wayside and successes passed on through the generations.

Early humankind did not have metal tools and fasteners, but they did have excellent stone tools, and quality timber framing could and would have evolved without metal. Archaeological evidence at Neolithic sites — post holes primarily, as little wood has survived — show the shapes of houses in Europe 5,000 years ago, and suggest the kind of rafter systems that would have been required to roof the structures. Some were quite magnificent, like the huge round wooden temple at Stanton Drew in Somerset, England, which predates the megalithic stone circle at the same site. This earlier structure, discovered by the use of magnetometers in the late 1990s, would have had a diameter of 312 feet (95 meters), and was composed of about 400 very large oak posts. Experts disagree as to whether or not it was ever roofed, but the radial location of posts strongly suggests a radial rafter system. A project of this scale, at that time of much lower population than today, was an infinitely more impressive feat than, say, the building of London's Millennium Dome or a modern American indoor sports arena.

How long these buildings lasted we shall never know. We know now that longevity of a wooden structure is closely tied to the quality of the foundation and the roof. The primary cause of wood rot is the propagation of fungi, which require air, water, and nutrients. If a constant damp condition can be avoided, wooden buildings will last an awfully long time. You need "good shoes and a good hat," said the old-time builders, referring to the foundation and roof. I would add, "and good ventilation."

As a youth of 19, visiting the Alpine village of Wengen, Switzerland in 1967, I was asked to guess the age of the large chalet where I stayed. The building looked new, but I dutifully guessed an age of twenty years. I was shocked to learn that the home was 500 years old. The alpine climate, the quality of construction, and Swiss maintenance combined to preserve the building in an "as-new" state.

An example of this craftsmanship is worth relating. Wood swells at humid times, and shrinks when the air is dry. There's not a great deal we can do about it. Nailed-down hardwood floors can buckle when they take on moisture, for example. In some Swiss houses of centuries past, the floorboards were not nailed down. Rather the center plank (or more than one) in the floor were tapered, with their ends actually sticking out of the building, accessible to a wooden mallet. In the winter, when conditions were dry, driving the wedge-shaped boards in from one end tightened the floor. During humid times, the opposite ends of the boards could be struck with a mallet to slightly loosen the floor, thus preventing buckling. And just think of what an easy matter it would be to replace a board.

Timber Framing versus Standard Stud Construction

Most residential framing in North America today is done with stud construction — a light "stick frame" — often referred to as a platform frame, conventional frame or western frame. A "balloon frame," popular about 100 years ago, is a special type in which the vertical members, now known as studs, were quite long, spanning from first story right through the second story. This is uncommon now, with most stories built independently using the ubiquitous eight-foot stud.

Conventional stick-frame construction is typically fabricated with framing lumber having a thickness of just 1½ inches (3.8 centimeters). Vertical support studs are placed around the perimeter either 16 or 24 inches (40 or 61 centimeters) from the center of one stud to the center of the next one. Prior to 1924, frames were constructed with full "two-by" material. A two-by-four actually measured

two inches by four inches. Much of
this material came from small local
sawmills, and, in truth, the dimensions
of a two-by could vary by up to a
quarter inch. The local sawmills I
work with today are almost always
within an eighth of an inch of the true
dimension, and, very often, they are
spot on.

A nominal "two-by-four" today is
actually 1½ inches by 3½ inches. All
two-bys bought at large lumber
suppliers such as Lowe's and Home
Depot are 1½ inches thick. The actual
depth of a two-by-four is 3½ inches

Fig. 1.1: In 1975, the author, with his wife, Jaki, built Log End Cottage, West Chazy, New York, using simple timber framing strategies "for the rest of us." Panels between posts are infilled with cordwood masonry.

(8.9 centimeters), and the depth of a two-by-six is 5½ inches (14.0 centimeters).
After that, the true depth is three-quarters inch (2 centimeters) less than the
nominal dimension, so that a two-by-eight is 7¼ inches (18.4 centimeters) deep
and a two-by-ten is 9¼ inches (23.5 centimeters) deep. Sometimes, you can buy
"heavy timbers" at large building suppliers, such as six-by-sixes, but these, too,
lose one-half inch in the planer and have a true dimension of 5½ inches square.
It is important to know the difference between "rough-cut" (full dimensional)
timber and "finished" lumber, more commonly available.

This book does not discuss today's common stick-frame construction, because
there are already a number of excellent manuals on the subject that I cannot
improve upon. Some of these are listed in the Bibliography, but the list only
scratches the surface of what is available. Also, there are building schools that
teach this type of construction and they are noted in Appendix C. Many local
trade schools and technical colleges also offer courses in conventional building.

Rather, *Timber Framing for the Rest of Us* is meant to complement natural
building methods, in which the fabric of the building — cob, cordwood, straw
bale, waddle-and-daub, etc. — is essentially infilling between the heavy timbers
forming the building's structural framework. Also, the methods described herein
would be appropriate to storage sheds and barns where rough-cut lumber is to be
used as siding. Unlike conventional stick framing, which is based upon the use of
four- by eight-foot sheet goods, the center-to-center spacing of posts is typically

somewhere between six and ten feet (1.8 and 3 meters). This makes infilling much less tedious. Imagine trying to fill the narrow spaces in regular stud construction with cordwood masonry or straw bales.

People building heavy timber-frame structures do not normally buy much lumber at the large national lumber chain stores. Far more commonly, they will purchase their timbers from a local sawmill, make their own timbers with a chainsaw mill, or have a local sawyer visit their wooded property with a portable band saw, to have the standing trees converted to full-dimensional timbers. We'll look at these options in Chapter 3.

If lumber dimensions were the only consideration, it could be fairly argued that a full-sized 2-by-8-inch floor joist or roof rafter (16 square inches or 103.2 square centimeters) would be 47.12 percent stronger on shear strength than its store-bought equivalent that measures 1.5 inches by 7.25 inches, or 10.875 square inches (70.16 square centimeters). That sounds pretty good, and is true as far as it goes, but there are other considerations that contribute to a timber's strength.

Grading of Lumber: The Good, the Bad and the Ugly

Serious organic flaws such as large knots at the edge of a timber can greatly diminish both shear and bending strength. (I will explain the difference in Chapter 2, when the differentiation is more important.) Other defects are checks (shrinkage gaps), splits, and shake (separation of annual growth layers.) Shake weakens a timber considerably. This is where lumber grading becomes important. Trained lumber graders can certify a particular timber as being of a certain structural grade. However, the buyer must still be aware. At a meeting of sawyers I attended in December of 2002, an example was shown of a graded two-by-four stud purchased from a large building supplier. The grade stamp was clearly printed right on the stud. Because of poor quality, it took little effort to break the two-by-four in half by hand. The issue of using graded or non-graded lumber is a serious one and affects the owner-builder profoundly. Listen:

As I write, in early 2003, 48 of the 50 American states (including New York, where I live) have adopted the so-called International Building Code. (I say so-called because I cannot imagine that this 3-pound volume of codes would be of much use outside of North America.) One of the code requirements in this hefty volume is that all structural lumber be graded. Paragraph R502.1 says, "Load-bearing dimension lumber for joists, beams and girders shall be identified by a grade mark of a lumber grading or inspection agency that has been approved by an accreditation body that complies with DOC PS 20. In lieu of a grade mark, a certificate of inspection issued by a lumber grading or inspection agency meeting the requirements of this section shall be accepted." Paragraph R602.1 says the same thing with regard to "studs, plates and headers" and Paragraph R802.1 includes "rafters, trusses and ceiling joists." In short, all structural wooden components in residential structures in 48 states must be graded.

On December 3, 2002, an emergency meeting of small sawmill owners came together near Lake Placid, New York, to discuss this provision, which was due to take effect on January 1, 2003. Most of the 200-odd attendees were rural sawyers, who, rightly, saw this new code as threatening their livelihood.

What happened next was a lesson of democracy in action. From all over the state, representatives of various sawmill and rural associations, supported by state senators and assemblymen, went to Albany to attend and speak at the December 11th meeting of the New York State Code Council. The code council unanimously adopted a proposal by the Empire State Forest Products Association in concert with the Department of State and the New York State Department of Conservation to reinstate a "local option" regarding grade stamping for structural lumber.

Hundreds of letters and thousands of signatures on petitions helped turn the tide on this issue. According to a press release sent to me as a petitioner, the upshot is that now, as before, "Rough cut lumber can be used for structural purposes if the code enforcement officer allows it and the mill guarantees that the lumber meets minimum (grade 2 or better) standards. The mill will be required to sign a form that will be provided by the local code officer and this form will need to accompany the building permit application. These provisions apply to residential construction not exceeding three stories in height, and all other buildings not exceeding 10,000 square feet in area or 35 feet in height."

Over the past several years, three or four of our students at Earthwood Building School have reported difficulty in using their own lumber or locally sawn lumber in the construction of their own homes, the local code enforcement officer insisting in each case that the lumber be professionally graded. The cases I have heard about have occurred in Michigan and Ontario, but it could happen almost anywhere in North America now, so the owner-builder needs to be aware. The sidebar on page 10 tells the story of Mark Powers' battle for a permit in Michigan. His experience is by no means singular, and the wisdom he has garnered — and shares with us — may be valuable to the next owner-builder facing a similar hurdle.

Making the Grade

Mark Powers, owner-builder, Alanson, Michigan

Upon hearing that I planned to build a timber frame home with an earth roof, the immediate response from the building department supervisor was, "Are you a structural engineer? I'm not." I knew then that I would have to hire an engineer. But another problematic issue soon arose, revolving around the fact that I was felling my own trees (hardwood, no less) and chainsaw-milling them into posts and beams. The issue concerned the use of ungraded hardwood lumber.

Finding an engineer was a process by itself, as I encountered resistance to the idea of using native timbers. Many engineers simply don't want to be bothered with "gray" areas when it comes to what they think of as unconventional building.

Tracking down someone to grade my homespun hardwood timbers was even more difficult than finding the right engineer. We live in the northern part of Michigan's lower Peninsula. Numerous local sawmills process the fine maple, oak and beech stands in our region, but none of the ones I contacted graded hardwood for its structural properties, but only with respect to veneer lumber, flooring, and the like. I contacted a "certified" hardwood lumber grader through one of the mills, who made a 90-mile round trip to my place only to reveal that he didn't know how to grade posts and beams for structural purposes. So I cast my net further afield.

The Department of Forestry at Michigan State University referred me to the National Hardwood Lumber Association (NHLA) in Memphis, Tennessee. Through them I connected with a sympathetic inspector who proposed an alternative to having him visit my location and charging me the minimum fee of $470 a day, plus expenses. He volunteered to call the local "certified" inspector — the one who had already visited — and explain to him how to grade hardwood for structure. The grading was done according to guidelines from the Northeastern Lumber Manufacturers Association (NeLMA) in Maine. The inspector charged me $120 and apologized that the bill came to that much. It seemed quite reasonable to me, considering the time he spent educating himself to "make the grade."

Incidentally, the building inspector was not the only one who needed the certified grading; my engineer also needed it in order to feel comfortable about assigning values to my timbers. Thankfully, my building inspector is basically on my side and seems to appreciate the lengths I've gone to satisfy code. I've maintained a cordial relationship with all the inspectors I've dealt with, and though it's been mighty frustrating at times, the good will is generally repaid in kind. It pays dividends to treat the building department as a resource, and not an adversary.

Author's note: The two lumber organizations mentioned above, NHLA and NeLMA, are listed in Appendix C.

In short, the grading of lumber can be an expensive proposition, which defeats the advantage of using local rough-cut lumber in the first place. At this time, despite widespread adaptation of the International Building Code, it is possible for most people in rural areas to build with non-graded lumber. Check on this with the town or county building inspector before placing a big lumber order with your local sawmill, or cutting quantities of your own lumber with a chainsaw mill. If evasion is a strategy that you have in mind — I am not advocating this, you understand — then you might want to gain the information anonymously.

My guess is that wherever the local forest products industry is strong, there will be (or soon will be) provisions such as the one recently adopted by New York to allow the use of rough-cut lumber. Economic considerations aside, you cannot easily purchase heavy timbers from ordinary building supply yards. Local sawmills, farm sawmills, and personal timber cutting (small chainsaw or bandsaw mills) are the realistic and affordable choices, and these are discussed in Chapter 3.

Timber Framing: Advantages and Disadvantages

Whether you go with "traditional" timber framing (which the Timber Frame Guild likes to call "contemporary timber framing") or "timber framing for the rest of us," certain advantages and disadvantages are common to both systems.

Strength. Timber framing by either method is strong. It is not only strong in real structural terms, but it exudes a sense of strength in the architecture. It is hard to visit a half-timbered framed house or country pub in England and not be impressed with the atmospheric power of the structure, a power that owes much of its strength to the visual impact of the beautiful exposed timbers, especially the big old gnarled ones.

Heavy-timber frames, with or without infilling, are more resistant to trauma from earthquakes, wind uplift, and snow load than light-frame construction. In areas prone to these natural calamities, care must be taken to meet local building code with regard to tying the frame to the foundation, as well as the roof to the frame.

Conducive to infilling. As already stated, heavy-timber framing is more appropriate than stick framing as regards infilling with the various natural building methods popular today. With infilling, it is not critically important that exactly 14½ inches (36.8 centimeters) is left between vertical members, either studs or posts. Masonry and cob can fit any space. Straw bales can be made to fit

Fig. 1.2: Ki Light built a straw bale house near West Chazy, New York using a simple timber frame whose members are joined by the non-traditional means described in this book.

almost any width of space, too, if the baling twine is retied as described in various straw bale construction manuals.

Esthetic appeal. Normally, timber frames are left exposed, either on the interior, the exterior, or, in many cases, on both sides of the wall, such as the guesthouses and the garage at Earthwood. With many of the professionally built contemporary timber frame houses, structural insulated panels are fastened to the outside of the frame, and the beautiful heavy timbers are left exposed on the interior. (see Sidebar on page 13) At some 16-sided cordwood homes, the heavy timbers are in evidence on the exterior, but not on the interior. Chapter 6 of my previous book *Cordwood Building: The State of the Art* [see Bibliography] contains a detailed description of this almost-round timber frame. The method is of most interest to cordwood masonry builders, and is not repeated in this work.

In all cases, the exposed timbers lend character, texture, and an esthetic sense of strength to the architecture. All of this translates into comfort, spiritual and otherwise.

Ease of construction. If you've never built anything before, you might actually find timber framing to be easier than conventional studding, which requires fairly exact tolerances for the application of sheetrock, plywood and the like. With timber framing, there are far fewer pieces to handle. And tolerances, at least in the post and beam frame, do not need to be quite so exact, particularly when the walls are infilled with natural materials. True, much of the work will require two people, but this is also true with stick-frame construction.

Economy. If you are buying from a local sawmill or a farmer, or if you are making timbers from your own trees, timber framing is almost certain to be more economical than buying finished lumber. When buying heavy timbers from a distant source, this advantage is lost and timber framing may become more expensive. The key to building anything economically by any method is to use local or indigenous materials.

Structural Insulated Panels

Structural Insulated Panels (SIPs) are foam-core panels that can either stand alone in place of stick-frame construction, or can be mounted to the exterior of a timber frame to provide a continuous wrapping of insulation. Think of an ice cream sandwich. The inner and outer surfaces (the chocolate wafer) of this sandwich are oriented-strand board, commonly known as OSB. The vanilla ice cream part is composed of rigid foam insulation, commonly either EPS (expanded polystyrene) or urethane foam. Any common interior or exterior finish can be applied, such as clapboard, gypsum board, stucco, and so forth.

Another common term you will hear is stress skin panels, also known as curtain wall panels. These panels are non-structural, a little less expensive than SIPs, and can be used with timber framing, although most timber framers just go with the more rigid SIPs, because cabinets and other components can be readily fastened to SIPs, but not to the non-structural panels.

Doug Anderson of Winter Panel Corporation in Vermont (see Appendix C) tells me that the stress skin panels are often chosen as a roofing panel, as they will span up to four feet in an area with a 40 PSF (pounds per square foot) snow load. With greater snow loads or greater spans, SIPs are used. Stress skin panels commonly have gypsum board on the interior instead of OSB.

Prior to the advent of SIPs and stress skin panels over the past twenty years, timber framers would stud out the spaces between posts and insulate with fiberglass, a labor intensive, time-consuming process which was not nearly as good as an insulation barrier. See Appendix C for SIP resources and the Bibliography for an excellent book on the subject.

"Traditional" Timber Framing

I use the term "traditional" timber framing to describe the system of joining timbers to each other without benefit of metal or mechanical fasteners. Typically, posts, girders, rafters, king and queen pins, etc., are connected to each other by the use of time-tested joinery such as mortise and tenon joints, scarf jointing, dovetails, rabbetting, etc. A good example of traditional timber framing is seen in Figure 2.17, in the next chapter.

In most cases, one or more people will lay out the various sides, gable ends, and "bents" (internal wall framing or other internal structural assemblies) on the ground. Time and care are taken to join the various heavy timbers by one of the many clever and intricate joints that have evolved over the centuries. Sometimes, particularly with owner-builders, a completed section will be raised with the help of friends, so that there is room on the site (or foundation slab) to build the next component. Alternatively — and this is more common with experienced timber frame builders — the entire barn or house frame may be erected in a single day. Professionals often manufacture all of the components in a shop environment, making sure that the pieces fit together properly, and then reassemble the frame on site.

Although traditional timber frames are sometimes used with natural infill alternatives, they are more commonly built to support pre-made insulated panels on the exterior, with wooden siding installed later. The fine joints are in evidence on the internal skeleton of heavy timbers, a beautiful and impressive effect. Spacing of vertical members is more critical when applying manufactured stress skin panels than it is when a natural infilling is used between posts. See Appendix C and the Bibliography for resources about stress skin panels, and structural insulated panels.

Done professionally, traditional timber framing can be quite expensive because of the labor and materials cost, but good timber framers are worth every cent they get in terms of quality. Owner-builders can do the work, too, but developing and using the required skills will add very much more time to the project. I am an experienced owner-builder, but I would certainly take a two-week course at one of the building schools before embarking on a traditional timber-framing project.

Timber Framing for the Rest of Us

Strong, functional, and attractive timber-framed buildings are made by farmers, carpenters, and owner-builders throughout the world, and only a small proportion of these projects involve traditional timber framing. Most of these rural buildings — even houses, when heavy timbers are used — involve the use of truss plates, joist hangers, pole-barn nails, log cabin spikes, gravity, screws, bolts and ingenuity. These builders learn from their neighbors, family, local builders, and sometimes just by asking advice at the local sawmill or lumberyard. It's sort of like the way beavers and other building species learn their trade.

But sometimes it's hard to find someone to help on the project, so here we are. Now we need to talk about some basic structural principles.

CHAPTER TWO

Basic Timber Frame Structure

My FATHER WAS A MECHANICAL ENGINEER. When we kids had difficulty learning how to coordinate the clutch with changing gears, he would explain to us the mechanics of what was actually taking place inside the transmission, and that seemed to make learning to shift a whole lot easier. We could visualize the nasty things that would happen if the clutch were not engaged before changing gears. You don't need to know anything about clutches to build a timber frame, but in a similar way, knowledge about a few basic principles of structure will help you to prevent nasty things from happening to your building.

Load and Line of Thrust

Any structure has to support itself and anything that is added to it, such as furniture, people, earth, snow, even wind. All of these things fall under the general category of load, but the term should be broken down even further.

The dead load or structural load is the weight of the structure. First, a building must be able to support itself.

The live load is the total of the forces acting on the frame as a result of its use, such as furniture, people, items in storage, and the like.

The snow load is a specific live load, which varies from place to place. It is the weight of the maximum accumulation of snow that can be expected in your area. Check with the local building department. Plattsburgh, New York, for example, uses a snow load of 70 pounds per square foot (PSF).

Wind load is different in that it is not predicated upon weight. We can set it aside for a moment, but it is important and we will return to it in Chapter 4, page 75, under the heading *Wind Can be a Serious Problem*.

Those living in earthquake zones will need to consider yet another load, a lateral live load that occurs as a building oscillates during a tremor. In a severe quake, this lateral load can be more severe than wind loading. Check with your local building department if you live in a seismic zone.

The resultant or combined load is the total effect and resulting direction of all of the various loads that act on a structure. We'll see an example of this when we discuss the several different loads on an earth roof.

Sam Clark, author and professional builder, explains the business of a structure in a very clear way:

> To withstand the loads on it, a house structure must meet three criteria. One, the individual members of the structure, such as beams, joists, and studs, must be strong enough. Two, the members must be attached to one another properly. The joints must be strong. Three, the lumber must be assembled so that the structure as a whole is rigid. (Clark, 1996.)

A term frequently used in discussions of stress in structure is the line of thrust or thrust line, which can be thought of as the transfer of a load. Structural design deals with thrust lines so that the building is kept in a state of static equilibrium, which, with timber framing, often consists of balancing compression and tension forces.

Figure 2.1 shows the various loads on a section of a simple gable-roofed structure. With the exception of the wind load, most of the line of thrust from the roof is downward, following gravity. But the weakness of such a building is in its joints: the connection between rafters or roof surfaces at the ridge, and the connection of the rafters or roof surface with the posts or sidewalls.

As drawn, the combined roof load will impart tremendous lateral stresses on the sidewalls, causing them to spread and, ultimately, to fall over, as shown in Fig. 4.37a, on page 88 of Chapter 4. Neither the most skilled timber joinery nor the best metal connectors can be expected to last long under these circumstances. The problem is bad design.

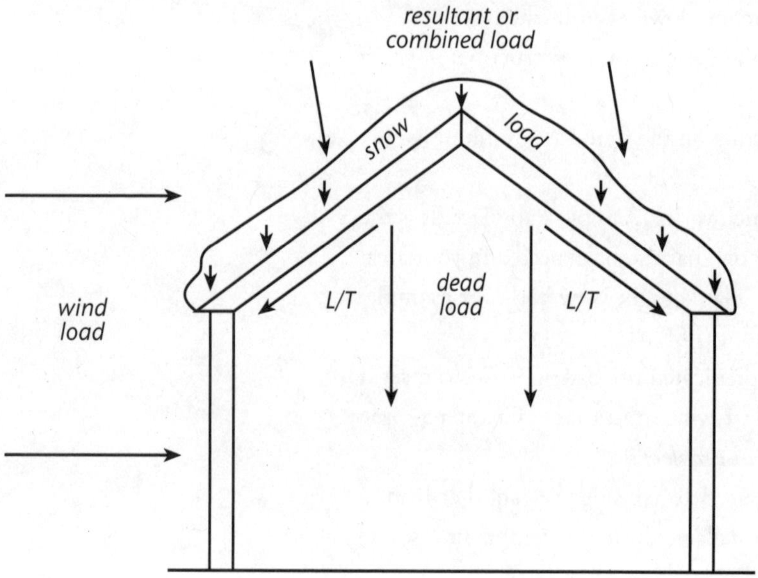

Fig. 2.1: The various loads in this structure put great strains on the jointing. The line of thrust — marked L/T — transfers the resultant load most easily by spreading the sidewalls. This event is simply a matter of time and could even happen during construction.

resultant or combined load

snow   load

wind load

L/T   dead load   L/T

While you've got your finger on page 88, check out Figures 4.37b and 4.37c, which show two good ways to make this weak structure much stronger. We'll revisit these particular structural considerations, as they relate to actual building, in Chapter 4.

Compression

Compression — in wood, not my father's car engine — can be thought of as the tendency to crush or compress under a load. The actual crushing or compressing does not have to be measurable to be real. If I stand on a stout — say, 12-inch diameter by 12-inch high — oak chopping block, my weight puts that chopping block in compression, even though I am having no measurable impact upon it. My entire family could balance atop the block to no effect, yet the block is definitely in compression. It might seem that such a stout block would never fail under compression, and yet it can under extreme circumstances. In October of 2003, Jaki and I rotated a 20-foot long 20-ton stone on a 12-inch-wide pivot made of a dense hardwood, an incredible concentrated load. Yes, the pivot eventually failed — it was crushed and ruptured apart, finally — but we did manage to swing the stone through almost 90 degrees of arc before it did.

The stresses on posts or columns are due mostly to compression, particularly if the line of thrust from above is straight down through the center of the post, as in Figure 2.2a. (Our chopping block example, incidentally, is simply a short stout post.) However, if the line of thrust wanders out of the middle third of a post — or a wall — then the side of the post or wall where the load is concentrated is in compression, while the side away from it is in tension. (Fig. 2.2b).

Fig. 2.2a: The line of thrust is in the middle third of the wall. The reactionary thrust is in compression.

Fig. 2.2b: The line of thrust has wandered into the outer third of the wall, still under compression, but the inner surface is on tension and the wall is unstable.

Fig. 2.2c: The line of thrust has left the confines of the wall, which now buckles and fails.

Tension

Tension can be thought of as the opposite of compression. While compression wants to squish the molecules of a material together, tension is trying

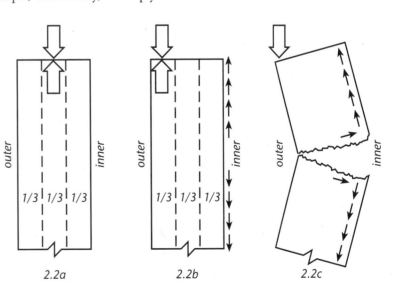

2.2a   2.2b   2.2c

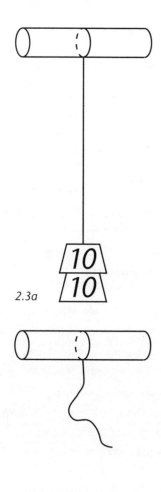

2.3a

2.3b

Fig. 2.3a Tension. and 2.3b.
Tension failure.

to stretch the molecules apart. If I hang lead weights on a string, the string is in tension. If I keep adding more lead weights until the tensile strength of the string is exceeded, we will observe a failure in tension: the string breaks.

If the line of thrust actually leaves the edge of the support structure, as per Fig. 2.2c, the member will hinge somewhere along its height and something — like the upper story or the roof — will come crashing down.

While writing the above paragraph, I envisioned a building failing in the way described. It happens, particularly with old abandoned buildings under a severe load, such as heavy snow or strong wind. It occurred to me that the failed building lands up in some kind of an untidy heap, which, in and of itself, is actually a new structure, one designed instantly by the physics that apply near the surface of this planet. If you looked carefully at the resultant pile of twisted and broken timbers, you would see a structure with new lines of thrust being distributed along tension and compression, and by way of natural triangles and trusses. Such a pile might be weak, only able to support itself for a short time, or it might be surprisingly strong. An old barn building near us has been slowly receding into the landscape for 25 years.

We'll talk more about posts later, but I think it would be helpful to consider beams first, because posts, surprisingly, share some of the same characteristics as beams.

Compression and Tension in Beams

Beam is a good catch-all word to identify a (usually) horizontal timber whose job it is to carry a load across a span. Girders and floor joists are common specific examples, as are lintels over doors and windows. Even though many roof rafters are pitched to some degree, they perform as beams, too, although other thrust considerations come into play.

Let's load a simple but imaginary beam to see how it works. We'll make it a rather flimsy beam so that its exaggerated performance will show what's happening. Imagine a 12-foot long two-by-eight plank spanning — flatwise — from one support to another. If the ends of the plank are each bearing on a foot-wide concrete block, the clear span between supports is ten feet. Now I'll step on to the center of this "beam," rather carefully, with my 170-pound weight. Obviously, the plank sags in the middle, and quite a bit. But it probably doesn't break, even though it has me a little worried. What is happening is that the underside of the plank is being stretched under my weight; that is, it is in tension. At the same time, the molecules on the top surface of the plank are trying to crush together; it is in compression. Allowing that this is true — and it is — it follows that an imaginary line along the center of the plank's thickness is neither in compression nor tension. This line is known as the centroid or the neutral axis. See Fig. 2.4.

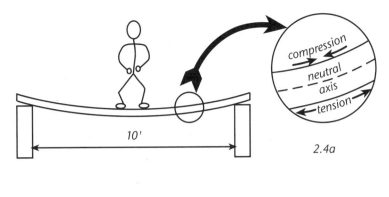

An imaginary beam as here described would be very springy, somewhat like a trampoline. Move one of the supports inward four feet, and we are on the way to

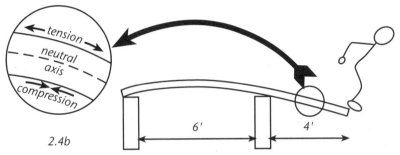

inventing both the cantilever and the diving board. Interestingly, when the beam is cantilevered by placing my weight at its free end, the top surface is now in tension and the bottom surface is in compression.

Instinctively, we know that to lay a "beam" flat like this is — well — stupid. Obviously, if the plank were rotated 90 degrees along its transverse axis — so that it looks like a proper floor joist — it would be very much stronger against bending pressures. It would feel quite stiff to walk along, providing I could maintain my balance for 10 feet. We may think that we know this instinctively, but I submit that it is a matter of our experience more than instinct.

Bending and Bending Failure

Yes, a good beam is a thing of beauty, but the main quality we are looking for in a beam is that it will not fail under the load we are asking it to carry. So we had better know a bit about the kinds of failures that can happen.

The failure in beams that people seem to grasp most easily is that of bending failure. If we keep loading a beam, particularly towards the middle of the span, we are placing ever greater bending stresses upon it. When we exceed the bending

Fig. 2.4a: Man on a plank, a simply-supported but flimsy beam.

Fig. 2.4b: Man at the end of his plank, a cantilever. A cantilevered beam is really an extension of a simply-supported beam and, unlike this picture, the inner — or non-cantilevered — portion is normally loaded or constrained by walls or a floor, which makes it stronger.

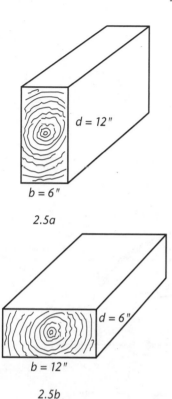

2.5a

2.5b

strength of the beam, it will break, usually somewhere in the middle third of the span. This seems logical and natural, just as it seems natural that the two-by-eight plank described above is far more likely to break under a bending load if it is laid flat than if it is installed, properly, on edge. But common sense aside, it is useful to know why this is so from a structural or mathematical standpoint.

Because of a strength characteristic with the rather imposing name of section modulus, the depth (d) of the beam — the vertical dimension — has its value squared. But the breadth (b) of the beam carries only a regular linear value. For beams with rectilinear cross-sections, section modulus (S) is expressed: $S = bd^2/6$. Interestingly, section modulus is solely a function of shape — geometry, if you like ... and not a function of materials.

This strength relationship can be shown clearly if we look at the example of a timber with a 6-inch by 12-inch cross-section, because the constant — 6 — cancels out so conveniently. In Fig. 2.5a, we see a section of a six-by-twelve beam installed as it should be. The section modulus is the breadth (b, or 6") times the depth (d, or 12") squared, all divided by the constant 6. $S = 6" \times (12")^2/6 = 144$ inches cubed, the unit for section modulus (not to be confused with cubic inches.) On the bottom (Fig. 2.5b), the beam has been installed by a builder, who, to put it kindly, "is as thick as two short planks." Now the breadth is 12 inches and the depth is 6 inches. So: $S = 12" \times (6")^2/6 = 72$ inches cubed. Now, mathematically, we can see that the beam is only half as strong in bending if we lay it down instead of standing it up correctly. I chose a six-by-twelve for easy math with whole numbers, but this relationship is true with any beam that is twice as deep as it is wide. With something like a two-by-ten joist, the difference is more extreme: the joist is five times stronger on bending installed "standing up" instead of "lying down." The section modulus for a truly square beam or girder, like an eight-by-eight or ten-by-ten, can make use of the same formula, but as b and d are the same, it can be simplified to $S = d^3/6$.

On Beams with a Round Cross-section, or Vigas

Many old barns and houses make use of floor joists and rafters that were made from locally grown straight tree trunks. Sometimes the builder would flatten one edge of the timber with an adz, so that roofing or flooring could be more easily nailed to it. In Mexico and the Southwest, exposed vigas (beams of round cross-section) are a common and attractive architectural feature.

Owner-builders today sometimes make use of their own home-grown timbers. They can be taken to a sawmill for squaring, they can be milled in the forest with a portable sawmill, or they can be barked and used in their natural round cross-sectional shape.

While this book is mostly concerned with the use of timbers milled on four sides, the author is in no way opposed to the use of viga-type beams, which can be quite beautiful. Here are some tips with regard to their use.

1. Choose sound straight trees for making vigas.

2. Remove the bark. The easiest time to do this is in the spring, when sap is rising. The greasy sap actually makes barking the wood very much easier, as it forms a slippery layer between the bark and the cambium wood layers. Good tools for barking include a pointed mason's trowel, a straight hoe, or a peeling spud made from any piece of flat stock metal that has an edge sharpened. Barking at the wrong time of the year, such as autumn, may necessitate the use of a drawknife, which is a lot like hard work.

3. For the purpose of judging the strength of a viga, consider its small end as the sectional dimension. Remember the old saying that a chain is only as strong as its weakest link? This principle is often appropriate with timber framing, where a mortise and tenon joint can actually reduce the shear strength of beams where they join a post. However:

Fig. 2.6: With rectilinear structures, alternate large and small ends of viga-type joists or rafters. The drawing is exaggerated to make the point.

4. For maximum strength with rectilinear structures, alternate large and small ends on parallel rafters or joists, as per Fig. 2.6. This is different from the weakest link analogy, as the entire floor or roof is distributed over several parallel rafters and alternating weak and strong members lends greater strength to the entire structure. Stronger members assist weaker members.

5. With a radial rafter system, where all the rafters or joists head towards the center, as in our round Earthwood house, put all the smaller ends towards the middle, where they are supported by a large post or a post-and-capital, as per Fig. 4.28. The frequency (space between members) is greater towards the center, so the strength there is naturally enhanced. The big ends are placed at the building's circumference, where they

help to support the greater planking spans and their resultant loads. Fig. 2.7.

Incidentally, for beams with a round cross-section, like vigas, the section modulus is expressed as $S = \Pi d^3/32$, or, simplifying constants, $S = .09818d^3$. So, for a beam cut from a tree trunk with a small-end diameter of eight inches, we get a section modulus of $.09818(8")^3$, or 50.27 inches cubed. A beam with a square cross-section, common with timber framing, has a section modulus of $S = d^3/6$. So, for a full eight-by-eight, $S = (8")^3/6 = 85.33$ inches cubed. I find it interesting that an 8" diameter log has so much less bending strength than an eight-by-eight timber. Also, the eight-by-eight is "stiffer." See the section on Deflection.

Fig. 2.7: With a radial rafter system, place the smaller end of the vigas over the center support post.

Shear and Shear Failure

Shear failure is much more difficult to envision than bending failure. In fact, with light frame construction, shear failure seldom comes into play, whereas it is an important consideration for heavy timber framing, particularly with a very heavy load such as an earth roof or a steam train.

One good way of explaining shear is to think of it as a combination of compression and tension stresses. Remember that the top surface of a beam is in compression, the bottom surface is in tension, and the centroid (middle part of the beam) is neutral (thus also called the neutral axis.) Fig. 2.8a shows the compression and tension forces at one end of a beam, where it is supported over a post or wall. The arrows show the compression and tension forces. Note that the arrows are pointing in opposite directions, and that the strength of the compression or tension forces diminishes closer to the neutral axis. Fig. 2.8b shows the kind of failure that can happen when the stresses in the beam cause the wood fibers to slide along each other at varying rates. Not surprisingly, the separations often follow annual growth rings. This is why woods prone to shake, such as hemlock, are also low in shear strength. (Shake is the term for a weakness in wood caused by separations between annual growth rings.) It is no coincidence that if a two-by-six hemlock plank is tossed too casually to the ground, it will shatter parallel to the grain.

Fig. 2.8a Left: White arrows indicate a heavy load on a beam supported by a post or wall. Horizontal arrows indicate compression (C) and tension (T) forces. The top of the beam is in compression and the bottom surface is in tension. The dotted line indicates the centroid or neutral axis. Fig. 2.8b Right: Shear failure occurs when adjacent layers of wood separate because of "sliding" forces (called "shear parallel to the grain") taking place in the wood, which make the beam much less resistant to heavy loads. This sliding is caused by differentials in compression and tension forces between one layer of wood and the next. This type of failure occurs near the beam's support.

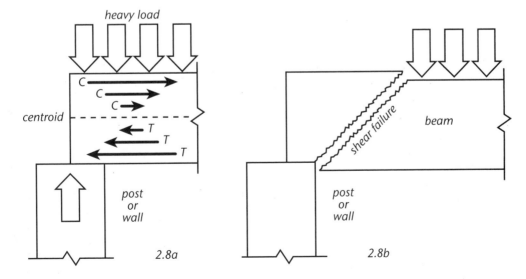

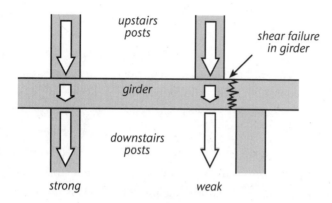

strong

weak

Fig. 2.9: The arrows indicate lines of thrust from the roof.

Some authors, without explaining the relationship between shear and tension and compression stresses, describe shear as the tendency for all of the wood fibers of the beam to "shear off," particularly at the edge of the post or wall support. While not complete, the analogy is true enough for our purposes, and may be easier to understand than lots of stress analysis. In Fig. 2.9, we learn a very important structural lesson. On the left, the line of thrust from the upper story is being transferred from the upstairs post, in compression though the girder, and down into the lower story post. Everything is in compression and wood is fairly strong in compression. (It is true that the concentrated load causes compression stresses on the girder and weakens it very slightly, but not enough to worry about.)

On the right side of the diagram, however, the line of thrust from above is not passed directly by compression to the lower post. The concentrated load from above misses the lower post in the most egregious way, almost begging for a shear failure near the edge of the lower post (or wall) as shown. Never do this!

Figure 2.10 shows a seemingly strange and certainly interesting situation, which we can use to our advantage. The top picture shows ten-foot long rafters bearing on walls at the edges of the building and over an eight-by-twelve internal

Fig. 2.10: Deflection is reduced with a double span as shown in the lower diagram, and bending strength is increased ... but shear strength is decreased by about 25 percent.

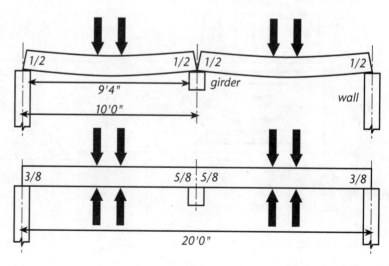

girder at the center of the building. If the rafters are bearing four inches onto the walls and girder, the clear span is actually 9 feet 4 inches (2.84 meters). In the bottom picture, we will use a 20-foot (6 meter) long rafter to do the same job.

The reader will probably not be surprised to learn that the situation at the top will promote more deflection in the rafters (deflection is discussed below) and will decrease the bending strength a little bit. The one-piece construction shown in the lower diagram "stiffens" the structure: greater bending strength and less deflection.

However — and this is the strange and interesting part — the structure at the top is actually stronger on shear. The structure in the lower part of the diagram has some very high shear stresses occurring on the top surface of the rafter where it passes over the girder. The effect of the sliding feature of the wood fibers over the neutral axis is increased, because the compression stresses on the top surfaces of the two spans are causing a tremendous tensile stress at the top of the rafter directly above the girder. Think of it: If the two spans are each trying to pull away from each other, because of the load on each span, those wood fibers at the top of the rafter (over the center) are working really hard not to break on tension. All of this translates to lower shear strength at this location. In the top picture, shear stresses over the supports are clearly the same at all four shear locations, expressed by the fractions ½ in each case. But, in the bottom picture, the shear stresses are expressed as ⅜ at the walls at the right and left but increase to ⅝ where the long rafter is supported by the girder in the middle.

The upshot is that shear strength is gained by using two ten-footers instead of a single 20-footer supported in the middle. It is also true, as we have said, that bending strength is slightly diminished in the former example, and deflection is increased — but if the weak point in the engineering happens to be in shear, the former example may be better. This situation may work in our favor, when you consider that two ten-footers are much easier to handle — and certainly less expensive — than a single twenty-footer.

Deflection

Deflection is similar to bending … but different. Bending concerns us most when it translates into bending failure, which is a bad thing. With deflection, we can tolerate certain amounts of it in certain circumstances. Springiness — or stiffness — in a floor is a characteristic of deflection. Cracking plaster on a ceiling, or separation of taped sheetrock joints, is an indication of excessive deflection.

Deflection is commonly expressed as a percentage or fraction of the span. Two common fractions you will encounter in span tables are $1/240$ and $1/360$ of a span. If a floor sags one inch over 240 inches (20 feet or 6 meters), this is a deflection of $1/240$. A half-inch sag in 180 inches (15 feet or 4.6 meters) is an example of a deflection of $1/360$. Charles Wing, author of several good books on homebuilding and sometimes called the father of the modern owner-builder movement, likes the $1/360$ rule for first floors, where, normally, you don't want to experience too much springiness.

There are also "rules" for ceilings. If you are supporting a plaster ceiling, deflection should be no greater than $1/360$. With gypsum board, taping, and spackling, you can get by with $1/240$ deflection. For roof rafters, a deflection of $1/180$ is normally allowable by code. (See author's note, p. 40.)

Personally, I don't use plaster or plasterboard ceilings, and I seldom use any kind of span greater than ten feet, because I put heavy earth roofs on almost every building I'm involved with. So, deflection has never been a big issue. With exposed plank ceilings, $1/180$ of deflection would be fine for roof rafters, and $1/240$ would certainly be acceptable for any floor with a wood ceiling beneath it.

Normally, if a floor joist or roof rafter plan meets the criteria for allowable loads on bending, it will be fine on deflection. Simply use commonly available span tables. I have included examples of some basic span tables in Appendix A, and also a list of where more comprehensive tables can be found. Here is just one example, to give you an idea of the kinds of dimensions we're talking about, and I get this right out of the new International Residential Code for One- and Two-Family Dwellings, Table R502.3.1(2), a portion of which is reproduced in Appendix A. We assume that this is a residential living area with a live load of 40 pounds per square foot (PSF), a dead load (structural load) of 10 PSF and an allowable deflection of $1/360$. Using Douglas Fir-Larch #1, and with joists 16 inches on center, a two-by-eight can span 13 feet 1 inch (3.99 meters). With two-by-tens, the allowable span increases to 16 feet 5 inches (5.0 meters). With a lesser quality of wood, such as #2 Southern Pine, the allowable spans drop to 12 feet 10 inches (3.91 meters) for two-by-eights and 16 feet 1 inch (4.90 meters) for two-by-tens. For residential sleeping areas, where loads of 30 pounds per square foot is assumed, allowable spans are greater. Find these figures in Appendix A, Table 1, and you will be well on your way to being able to use span tables.

Also in Appendix A, there are two examples of using a rafter span table with a 70-pound snow load and a 20-pound dead load. Back to posts …

We do not normally think of vertical members, such as posts or even trees, as being beams, but, in fact, they share a lot in common with beams. The word "beam" even comes from an old English word meaning tree or tree trunk. When a tree is being blown by the wind, the windward side is in tension as the tree bends away from the wind. The leeward side is in compression. Actually, as the tree is unsupported at the top, it can be

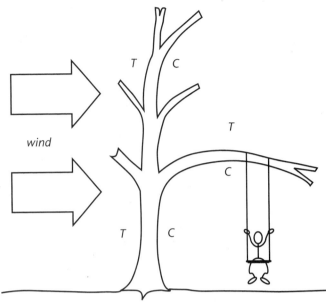

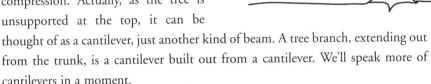

Fig. 2.11 The "frame" of a tree. Post? Beam? Cantilever? All of the above? T and C indicate Tension and Compression stresses.

thought of as a cantilever, just another kind of beam. A tree branch, extending out from the trunk, is a cantilever built out from a cantilever. We'll speak more of cantilevers in a moment.

In "post and beam" construction, the posts are the naturally strong component, because they are extremely strong on compression. For example, a six-by-six of a relatively low compressive strength of 1,150 to 1,400 inch-pounds per square inch (you don't really have to know what this unit means to get the point here; I certainly don't) will support 32,800 pounds at eight feet of height. That's 16.4 tons! An eight-by-eight of the same quality will support 63,000 pounds, 31.5 tons.

Tons, I understand. Even with our two stories and heavy earth roof, five of the seven major eight-by-eight posts at Earthwood support about 10,000 pounds each and the other two (full-sized eight-by-eight solid oak) support only 15,000 each, way under their capacity. (An oak eight-by-eight is good for over 93,000 pounds at eight feet of height.) In short, the post part of "post and beam" framing is very strong.

Four-by-fours would actually do for five of the seven posts at Earthwood if it weren't for our esthetic sensibilities and something called "slenderness ratio" or SR. Visually, a four-by-four supporting an eight-by-eight or ten-by-ten girder just doesn't look right, like a four-by-eight rafter laid the wrong edge down. But, structurally, the four-by-four post would probably do the job.

Fig. 2.12: This garage, based on our garage design at Earthwood, was built by Chris Ryan. Put windows on the gable end instead of a garage door and it becomes a charming cottage.

"Slenderness ratio" is simply the relationship of the width of the post its length. A 96-inch (8-foot or 2.44-meter high) post that is only four inches wide on its narrowest dimension has an SR of 96 inches/ 4 inches, or 24. Put an eight-by-eight there, and the SR becomes 96 inches/ 8 inches, or 12. The higher the number, the weaker the post. A slender post is much more subject to buckling than compression failure. Let's say we had a four-by-four supporting a heavy load as a post, and that there was a large knot on one or more edges of the post. While knots can be fairly strong in compression, they are weak in tension, as they tend to separate easily from the surrounding wood. A lateral load, such as a sudden impact, or the oscillation during an earthquake, could easily cause such a post to buckle and fail. Extreme vertical loads could do it, as well.

Post and Beam Frame

The "beam" component of "post and beam" timber framing usually refers to a heavy top plate, sometimes called a girt, or it could refer to a girder. Girts will often be supported later by infilling the individual panels of the building's perimeter. In this book, I use the word "panel" to refer to the spaces between posts around the perimeter. Girts can also gain strength by the use of intermediate posts, between the major posts. If not called upon to provide a joining surface for two consecutive girts, these intermediate posts can be less substantial, thus less expensive. An example of this is our garage at Earthwood. See Figures 2.12 (photo) and 2.13 (post and girt plan.) We have full-sized eight-by-eights at each corner of the 24-foot by 28-foot (7.3-meter by 8.5-meter) structure. In addition, we have eight-by-eights halfway along the walls. But, providing further strength to the girts, we have what I think of as secondary posts, still substantial four-by-eights, laid up so that the eight-inch (20.3 centimeter) dimension corresponds with the 8-inch thickness of the wall. The sides of the building, therefore, have four panels on the long side, each about seven feet in length including the posts, and also four panels on the south (gable) side, each about six feet long. The 24-foot-wide north side features a 16-foot garage door, with little four-foot panels on each side. An 18-foot-long (5.48-meter) eight-by-eight carries the girt system over the garage door. This large beam can also be thought of as a giant lintel over the garage door.

I was told at a building supply that the rough opening for our double garage door was 8 feet high and 16 feet wide, and it was framed accordingly. In reality, the height dimension turned out to be seven, not eight, feet (2.13 meters). The door fit with a foot to spare. We later hung a horizontal two-by-eight from the eight-by eight with 10-inch pieces of two-by-eight material, filling the spaces with cordwood masonry. Because of this mistake, our garage is actually a foot higher than it needed to be, causing me to do a bit of extra cordwood work.

In the case of the girts at our garage, they were well-supported during construction, with temporary diagonals screwed to the external frame to prevent racking of the building due to wind loads. Later, individual diagonals would be removed and panels would be filled in with cordwood masonry, which also serves to prevent racking. We do not have any true girders at our garage, as we have at the Earthwood house. It is the clear-span girders in a post and beam frame that need to be engineered for both shear and bending. Appendix B gives an example of this.

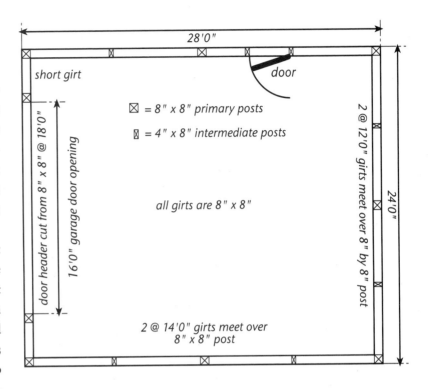

Fig. 2.13: Post and girt plan for Earthwood garage.

Plank and Beam

"Plank and beam" roofing (or flooring) is a structural system that is often combined with post and beam framing. The confusing part here is the use of the word "beam" in each case. For our generalized discussion, up to this point, it has been convenient to use the word beam, but now we must leave it behind in favor of more accurate —and therefore less confusing — terms. The "beam" component of the "plank and beam" system will be either a floor joist or a roof rafter, not girts or girders.

Just as posts are the naturally strong part of a post and beam frame, it is the planking that is the strong component of the plank and beam system. To give you an idea of just how strong planking can be, two-by-six tongue-in-groove decking can easily support a heavy (eight-inch or 20.3-centimeter thick) earth roof and a 70-pound snow load, with supporting rafters at four feet (1.2 meters) on center (48 inches o.c.). The earth roof described, with dead (structural) load comes to about 170 pounds per square foot. Conventional roofs in our area are required to support 70 pounds per square foot.

So engineering problems will not be found in the strong planking. The situation described in the preceding paragraph calls for some extra heavy-duty girders and rafters to support such an earth roof if the rafters are 48 inches on center. By the way, with a parallel rafter system the term "on center" refers to the distance from the center of one rafter to the center of the next. With normal framing, on-center spacing of floor joists is typically 12 inches (30.5 centimeters), 16 inches (40.6 centimeters), or 24 inches (61 centimeters). With heavy timber construction, other on-center spacing may be appropriate. At our Log End Cave earth-sheltered house, it was convenient to use a spacing of 32 inches (81.3 centimeters) on center. This worked out well with the predominantly eight-foot (96-inch) planks we used.

The number of rafters used, a function of the on-center spacing, is also known as the frequency of the rafters. The strength of the roof system (all else being equal) is a direct linear function of the frequency. If "direct linear function" throws you, think of it by way of a simple example. If you double the number of rafters (with spans, loads and rafter quality staying the same), you will, in fact, double the strength. You will be able to support twice the load with twice as many rafters by placing rafters on 12-inch centers instead of on 24" centers. This is an easy, if expensive, way to increase the shear and bending strength of a roof system.

Some Typical Loads, in Pounds per Square Foot (PSF)

Attic, where finished rooms are not a possibility =	20 PSF
Bedrooms =	30 PSF
Living areas =	40 PSF
Snow load — variable — ask local building inspector =	10 to 100 PSF
Fully saturated earth (10 PSF per inch of thickness, thus 8 inches = 80 PSF) =	10 PSF per inch
Crushed stone: Same as saturated earth (10 PSF) =	10 PSF per inch
Conventional roof framing with roofing and insulation =	7–10 PSF*
Heavy timber framework, roofing and insulation for an earth roof =	About 15 PSF*

* Note: this is the dead load. With conventional (non-earth) roofing, the dead load is included in the rafter span tables. Thus, if you are looking at a table for rafters for a zone of 70-pound snow load, the dead load is also factored into the table. With heavy frames, such as for earth roof construction, it is better to add the dead load to everything else.

Design Considerations for Rafters and Girders

As we have seen, the posts and the planks are the strong components of the post and beam (post and girder) and plank and beam (plank and joist or rafter) systems. The use of posts in scale with the girders will assure post strength. Two-by-six tongue-in-groove planking is an excellent and pleasing floor and roof system, although you should know that the true finished dimensions of this material is actually 1½ inches thick by about 5⅛ inches wide. With frequent joists or rafters, you can easily use the lighter and less expensive "five-quarter" (full one-inch) by six-inch (5⅛ inch) tongue-in-groove planking. In reality, you can use three-quarter-inch plywood, even with an earth roof, as we did at our library. We had no sagging at all, though the greatest span on the radial rafter system was only about 39 inches (99 centimeters), and this was on the overhang.

The members that need to be engineered for are the girders, the rafters, and the floor joists. It is important to know that there are five distinct considerations that come into the design work for these members, and they are:

1. **Load**. You have to know what degree of load you are asking the system to support. (See Sidebar on page 31.) So, as an example, if you are planning an eight-inch-thick thick earth roof over a two-inch-thick crushed stone drainage layer, for an area with a 70-pound snow load, add the following figures from the chart: 80 (earth) + 20 (stone) + 70 (snow) + 15 (dead load) = 185 PSF.

2. **Wood quality**. To engineer for any beam, you have to know the stress load values for the species and grade of wood you plan to use, particularly the unit stress ratings for bending and for shear (in pounds per square inch). For example, unit stress for bending can vary from 1,100 PSI (Eastern Hemlock, common structural) to 2,150 PSI (Douglas Fir, inland region, select structural).

3. **Frequency of rafters or joists**. As discussed above, under the heading Plank and Beam (page 29), frequency simply refers to how many members you are using. Are the rafters on 16-inch centers? 24-inch centers?

4. **Beam dimensions in section**. Will you be using two-by-eights? Five-by-tens? Eight-by-eights? Vigas with a small-end diameter of six inches?

5. **Clear span of the beam**. This is the one that trips up most owner-builders, particularly when it comes to designing a structure to support an earth roof. The problem is that bending strength decreases as the square of the span. For example, let's compare a 10-foot span to a 20-foot span. Instinctively, many people think that a beam has to be twice as strong to support the longer span, other considerations remaining the same. There's a kind of logic there, but it is wrong. You've got to compare the squared spans. Ten times ten equals one hundred (10 × 10 = 100), but twenty times twenty equals four hundred (20 × 20 = 400). The beam carrying the 20-foot span needs to be four times stronger than the one carrying the 10-foot span.

I'm going to give another less obvious example of how span (squared) influences strength, an example that pops up all the time with students at our earth-sheltered housing classes. The stress-load calculations for both the Earthwood house and the "40 by 40 Log End Cave" plans are predicated upon nine-foot spans. These are popular designs that have been built all over North America. Invariably, people ask me if they can stretch the spans to ten feet. (Nine feet, I guess, seems just a little tight for them.) The answer is, of course, yes, you can do almost anything if you know what you're doing and you have enough money. Instinctively, people figure that rafters or girders probably have to be 10 percent stronger to carry the extra foot of span. The math says otherwise: $9 \times 9 = 81$. But $10 \times 10 = 100$. The difference is 19. And this difference must be expressed in relationship to the original 81, not 100. Well, my trusty calculator tells me that $19/81 = .23457$. The change will require making up a shortfall of about 23.5 percent, a considerable difference from the original engineering.

In the example above, the span has been changed, so one or more of the other four design considerations must be altered to make things right. We could decrease the load by 23.5 percent by using less earth and using a lightweight drainage product instead of a crushed stone drainage layer … or by building in Chattanooga instead of Buffalo to take advantage of the decreased snow load. We could choose a wood with 23.5 percent more bending strength, perhaps a stronger species or a higher grade of the same species. We could actually use 23.5 percent more of the originally engineered rafters by increasing the frequency, and that would take care of it. Or we could reengineer the sectional dimensions of the rafter; use six-by-tens instead of five-by-tens, for example.

You must know four of the five variables listed above to calculate the fifth. If you know load, quality of wood, rafter frequency, and span, for example, you can calculate the cross-sectional dimensions of the rafter. Or, given the kind and grade of wood, you can calculate the load that a particular rafter system will support.

If you can plug numbers into a formula, you may wish to follow through the examples of Appendix B: Stress Load Calculations for Shear and Bending. But, in reality, for more conventional (non-earth) roof systems, just use existing engineered span tables, like the one in Appendix A.

Cantilever

A cantilever, as in Fig. 2.4, can be thought of as an upside down beam, supported at just one end. It is "upside down" in the sense that its top surface is in tension while its bottom surface is in compression. Note that the unsupported part of the cantilever tends to impart the same kind of upside-down stresses as the supported part. I think of it as being a bit like a first-class lever: the downward pressure of

Fig. 2.14: The Mushwood Cottage.

the overhanging load pivots at the wall (which acts like a fulcrum) and causes an uplifting pressure on the supported portion.

During my researches, I have found writers (some of them engineers) who say that the over-hanging part should be one-third of the supported part. Others say 40 percent. Some say 50 percent is the absolute limit. Let us think of these numbers as parameters. Personally, I see no reason in house-building to exceed the one-third recommendation, and if there is a large load on the cantilever, I'd either consult a structural engineer or avoid the cantilever altogether.

At Mushwood, our summer cottage (Fig. 2.14), the second-story 29-foot (8.8-meter) diameter geodesic dome is supported by 16 radial four-by-eight joists, which, in turn, are supported by a 22-foot (6.7-meter) diameter cordwood masonry first story and a large post at the center of the building. The overhang of the dome by itself is 3½ feet (1 meter) beyond the outside edge of the cordwood wall, and the supported portion of the joist is 11 feet (3.35 meters). Dividing 3.5 by 11 gives 31.8 percent—not too bad at all, it would seem, but really it is not very good, as the dome is applying a concentrated load to the end of the cantilever.

In the case of a concentrated load, an overhang of 25 percent should be thought of as the limit (Clark, 1966, p. 189). However, Jaki and I wanted a three-foot walkway all around the deck, also to be supported by the radial rafters. Snow sliding off the dome accumulates on this deck, a heavy distributed load. If a lot of snow slides off the dome at once, we're looking at an impact load. Adding the 3-foot deck to the 3½-foot dome overhang, we have a total cantilever of 6½ feet (1.98 meters). The supported portion of the joist is still 11 feet. The new relationship is 6.5/11 = 59 percent, which exceeds anyone's rule of cantilever by quite a bit.

We attended to the problem by installing sixteen diagonal supports, which carry the line of thrust from the dome through the diagonals (which are in compression) to the floating slab foundation that supports the cordwood building. Now both the upstairs dome and the downstairs cordwood structure are floating on the slab. The cantilever, now, is just the 3-foot deck, which can be compared to the newly supported portion of the rafter, at 15½ feet (12 feet plus the 3½-foot dome overhang, supported by diagonal bracing.) The new math is 3/15.5 = 19.35 percent, well inside even the one-third rule. This has been perfectly fine for 12 years, even when a heavy snow slides down the dome and crashes to the deck.

Your Post and Beam Plans

If you are going to build your own home (or garage or barn or other outbuilding), why not design it yourself as well? In *Mortgage Free!* (see Bibliography), I go into lots of strategies for keeping costs down, but the strategy that I think is most

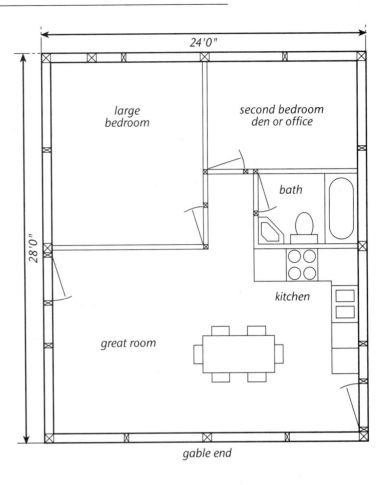

Fig. 2.15: The Earthwood-style post and beam garage frame is easily transformed into a cozy country cottage.

applicable to timber frame design is "Keep it Simple." Along these lines, consider fitting a floor plan to a simple structure, rather than drawing a floor plan and then trying to come up with a structural plan to fit it. Compromises between a simple structure and a floor plan that suits you can give you the best of both worlds.

As an example of this, I like to show how our simple and compact post-and-beam garage can just as easily be a charming but roomy one- or two-bedroom cottage. See Fig. 2.15, and have a glance back at Figures 2.12 and 2.13. Gross area (the way an assessor figures it) is just 672 square feet (62.35 square meters), about the size of a mobile home. Subtracting space "lost" in the eight-inch thick walls leaves 604 actual usable square feet. All internal walls are simply stud-framed partitions.

Traditional timber framers design their structures to make use of "bents." Steve Chappell, Director of Fox Maple School of Traditional Building defines a

Fig. 2.16: The principal members of this basic bent framing plan are the Posts, Tie Beam, and Rafters. The secondary members are the Interior Posts, Queen Posts, and Collar Tie. The secondary members are necessary only when bent spans exceed the structural limitations of any of the principal members. Braces are required to make this a rigid structural framework. These joints are made with fine crafted joinery, but such a bent could be constructed using mechanical fasteners and then raised into place. The drawing is by Steve Chappell, author of The Timber Framer's Workshop (Fox Maple Press, 1999), and is used with permission.

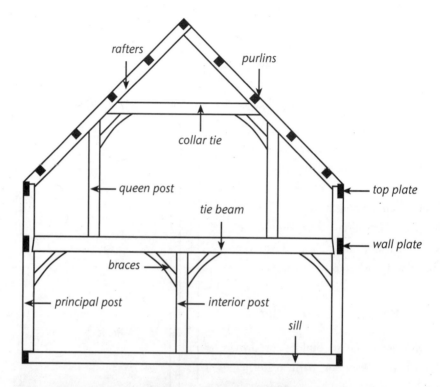

rafters

purlins

collar tie

queen post

tie beam

top plate

wall plate

braces

principal post

interior post

sill

Fig. 2.17: Students at Fox Maple School of Traditional Building in Brownfield, Maine, erect a timber frame at a workshop. Photo provided by Fox Maple Director Steve Chappell.

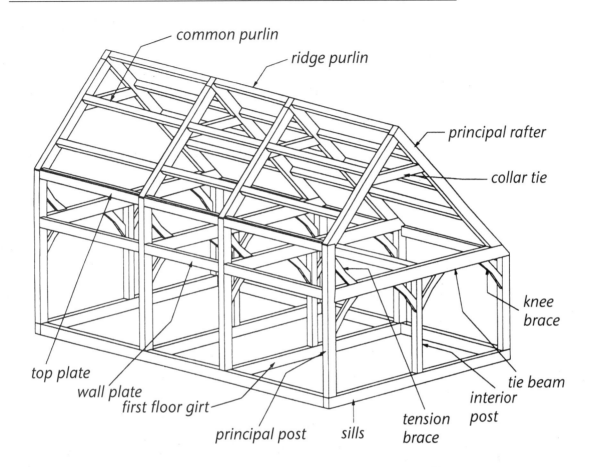

common purlin

ridge purlin

principal rafter

collar tie

knee brace

top plate

wall plate

first floor girt

principal post

sills

tension brace

tie beam

interior post

bent as "a transverse structural frame-work." Jack Sobon, author of *Build a Classic Timber-Framed House* (see Bibliography) describes a bent as "an assemblage of timber-frame components that can be put together lying flat and then reared up into position." He adds that bents are usually cross-frames, but adds that they can also be longitudinal wall frames.

There are no bents at our garage, in the sense of transverse frameworks, although the gable ends could have been built flat on the concrete slab and tilted up into position. The longitudinal sidewall framework could have been built that way, too. In the actual event, posts were simply stood up, individually fastened to the slab as described in Chapters 4 and 5, and the girts heaved into place and fastened together with connectors.

Fig. 2.16 shows a typical bent for a traditional timber frame. The installation of the top portion of such a bent is shown in Fig. 2.17. Four such transverse bents

Fig. 2.18: Parts of a traditional timber frame. This drawing is only intended to illustrate framing members. Other authors and timber framers might use slightly different terminology for some of the components. Drawing by Steve Chappell and used with permission.

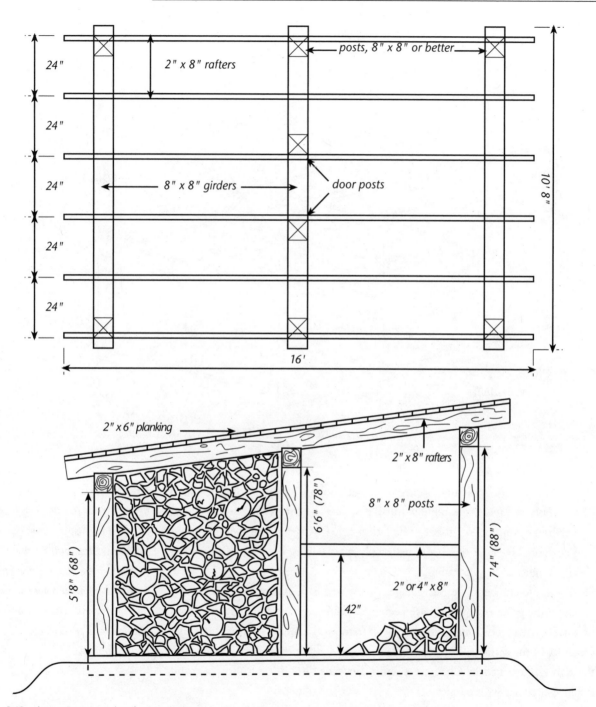

24"

24"

24"

24"

24"

24"

2" x 8" rafters

posts, 8" x 8" or better

8" x 8" girders

door posts

16'

10' 8"

2" x 6" planking

2" x 8" rafters

8" x 8" posts

6' 6" (78")

2" or 4" x 8"

42"

5'8" (68")

7'4" (88")

Fig. 2.19, above: Framing plan for Log End Sauna, Fig. 2.20, below: West elevation, Log End Sauna.

(two internal and one at each gable end) would be the major framework for a structure such as the one shown in Fig. 2.18, except that the upstairs of the frame in Fig. 2.18 is a little different; it is a saltbox design instead of the more common gable roof like Figures 2.16 and 2.17.

You could put a plank-and-beam roof on the lower frame of a building like our garage, but we chose pre-made engineered roof trusses to support our shingled roof. The convenience, economy, and strength characteristics of pre-built engineered trusses cannot be over-emphasized, and I will speak more of them in Chapter 4.

Fig. 2.21: The six posts are plumbed, then braced to stakes with scrap lumber.

There are as many timber frame plans as there are buildings. At one end of the scale, our little cordwood sauna design consists of just 6 major posts, 3 girders, and 6 long rafters, as per Figures 2.19, 2.20 and 2.21. At the other end of the scale are houses of 3,000 square feet and more.

You can design your own structure based on the design principles in this chapter, keeping in mind the various fastening techniques described in Chapters 4 and 5. Unless you are very confident of your own engineering capabilities — or are using a tried and proven plan — you should have a structural engineer check your plans. This is a lot less expensive than going to an engineer and saying, "Please design me a timber frame for this floor plan and such-and-such a snow load."

In New York State, any home of 1,500 square feet or greater must carry either an architect's or an engineer's stamp to get a building permit. (This takes the onus of responsibility off of the local building inspector.) Ki Light, a neighbor of mine, drew the plans for his post-and-beam house (with straw bale infilling) and took them to a local engineer to see if he could get his plans stamped. Ki and his wife spent a couple of hours with the man, and spoke of things like rafter frequency and span. "It took a while to explain straw bale construction to him," Ki told me, "but, as we'd be laying up the straw bales within a heavy post-and-beam frame, he was okay with it." The meeting cost the Lights $100. They received some good advice, and the engineer stamped their plans. In a couple of days they had their permit.

Another strategy that has worked well for some is to bring your seat-of-the-pants structural drawings to a college engineering class and have the class check and critique the plans … under the guidance of the professor, of course!

Finally, there are two sections in Chapter 4: Building Techniques, which also contribute to an understanding of structure. They are *Build Quality, Gravity and Inertia*, beginning on page 87, and *Roof Systems* beginning on page 88. I have put them there because they cover building techniques more than structure. But they are important enough to read now, and then again when you get to Chapter 4.

Now, you will need to know where you are going to get your timbers.

Author's note to the second printing

Geoff Huggins has observed, rightly, that stresses and deflection in cantilevered beams are reduced if some sort of constraint is supplied either over the beam supports (second storey walls or a roof for example), or as a distributed load along the beam (a heavy floor or ceiling). Further, Geoff comments that "the problems of deflection can be minimized if the structure is first built, beams are allowed to deflect, and then plaster or gypsum board is applied. The only additional deflection would be due to live loads, which are minimal."

CHAPTER 3

Procuring the Timbers

WHEN I WAS A YOUNG MASON'S LABORER IN SCOTLAND BACK IN THE 1970's, master stone mason Hughie Mathieson would say to me, "You cannae build without the stones, Robbie, you cannae build without the stones!" It was his way of telling me to get the lead out and provide him with more building stones on his scaffold.

With timber framing, you cannae build without the timbers! Now, where are they going to come from?

Recycled Timbers

Years ago, there used to be more old timber frame barns available for salvage than there are now. Jaki and I used lots of recycled barn beams at Log End Cottage, Log End Cave, and Earthwood. But, recently, a large barn became available. We heard about it through a friend. As Jaki and I didn't need timbers at the moment, and a young neighbor did, we put him onto this resource.

But even though the number of available barns has diminished, the use of recycled timbers is still a good strategy. Listen to Jim Juczak, who built a huge 18-sided timber-frame home (with cordwood infilling) near Watertown, New York:

The post and beam frame of our home is made out of recycled beams from a large bowling alley that was being demolished within six miles of our site. I asked the destruction foreman if I could get the wood from the 100-foot curved trusses that were being removed. I got ten of the huge trusses, 400 sheets of used ⅝-inch roofing plywood and about 500 pieces of 2- by 12-inch by 21-foot (6.4-meter) framing lumber. Our cost was $10,000 for what I estimated to be over $50,000 worth of materials. Disassembling the trusses, denailing the lumber, and deroofing the plywood took the better part of a summer. The curved pieces became roof rafters, the straight laminated pieces became the eighteen vertical posts in the outside wall and the four-by material became the radial floor joists for the second floor. The first floor was radially framed with the two-by-twelve-inch material and covered with two layers of recycled plywood.

Now, $10,000 may seem like a lot, but it supplied virtually all the structural, roof sheathing and flooring materials for a beautiful 3,000 square foot home. As Jim is skilled at scrounging materials like windows, doors, and even plumbing fixtures, the total cost of the home was only about $30,000 or $10 per square foot. Jim tells the full story of this project, with pictures, in my previous book *Cordwood Masonry: The State of the Art.*

Jim also gives a warning: "Unfortunately, getting all this great stuff into one place can be a detriment. Last June, someone with a housing need greater than my own felt compelled to 'borrow, without permission,' a tractor trailer load of salvaged construction lumber from our home site."

There are people in the salvage business who make a good living by tearing down old warehouses and the like, and selling the materials. In February of 2003, I had a lengthy and informative phone chat with my friend Bob Samuelson, a very successful dealer in recycled materials in the Chicago area. Bob built a 10,000-square-foot lodge in Wisconsin with huge timbers salvaged from Chicago warehouses that needed to come down. The walls are made from sixteen-by-sixteen-inch timbers, laid like logs. Internal posts are huge. Roof rafters are six-by-tens. Bob's comments were encouraging.

"Any city, small or major, has a demolition contractor, maybe several," Bob told me, "and there are plenty of timber frame materials being salvaged all the time. Also, more and more laminated timbers are becoming available. Use the internet or the Yellow Pages to find these contractors. And it's okay to gently bug them. They're nice people. If they see that you are trying to do something good for yourself, they will bend over backwards to help. There are around 3,000 demo projects a year, just in Chicago, but it's a small network and everyone knows everyone else. One person may not have what you want, but there's a good chance that they know someone who does."

Some demolition contractors may have recycled materials available, even old hewn timbers, but they are likely to charge a pretty penny for them, as they are in demand as atmospheric pieces in new restaurants and upscale homes. Bob says that Bill Gates of Microsoft fame used mostly recycled timbers on his big expensive house. You can't blame people for charging what the market will bear; they've gone to the trouble of doing the salvage work and need to be reimbursed for their time and effort. But, many of these contractors make their money from the actual demolition, not by selling the materials. They haven't got storage space to keep up with the rate of teardown. Bob tells me that with landfill charges of $400 to $600 a load, contractors are happy to find a cheaper way to get rid of materials, like bring them to you, for example. "You're helping them to clean their site," says Bob.

"Materials can be expensive or cheap and so can haulage, so shop around," Bob advises. "If you're not too far from the demolition site, the contractor might deliver to you fairly cheap, but if you are some distance away — say 250 miles or so from the site — expect to pay $400 to $500 for a semi load as a reasonable haulage charge."

Bob likes to speak in large units: "semi loads." A semi is a tractor-trailer unit, with, perhaps, a 50-foot (15.2-meter) flatbed trailer. Such a vehicle can carry up to 24 tons, which could be 12,000 to 15,000 board feet of lumber, depending on the density of the wood. This is enough lumber to frame — and complete — a good-sized home.

Bob had some other good tips. He mentioned that utility companies often have old cedar poles that they have replaced with new pressure-treated poles. Often times, only the large butt end (the part that went into the ground) was treated, usually with creosote. The rest of the pole might be in excellent condition and quite suitable for a viga-type rafter system, or tie beams, or internal posts. You can even flatten one or more sides, if you are careful to check the whole piece over for nails and spikes. A metal detector works well for this.

Summing up his commentary on salvaged material, Bob told me, "It's still there. Old buildings with great materials are coming up all the time, sometimes with virgin growth lumber you can't even get new."

For a bargain on recycled timbers, you are going to have to do some legwork (see Cultivating Coincidence below) or make the effort to find the old buildings and tear them down yourself, a strategy better suited for rural areas.

Tearing down old buildings is a lot more dangerous than building a new one. Heavy timbers can fall on you, and they don't shout a warning first. You can step on rusty nails, get poison ivy, or tangle with nasty dogs.

This is a book about building, not demolition, which is a whole different kettle of fish. The safest way to tear down an old barn, particularly one which is

The Board Foot

Whether you are dealing with the local sawmill or buying salvage, you need to be familiar with the term board foot, because that is the unit by which timber is sold.

A board foot (BF) is a square foot of wood one inch thick, or 144 cubic inches (2,360 cubic centimeters) of material. Every linear foot (LF) of a full one-by-twelve board is a board foot, but every linear foot of a full two-by-six is also a BF, because it also contains 144 cubic inches of wood (2 × 6 × 12=144). A linear foot (LF) is also called a running foot at many sawmills.

This lumber scale gives the number of board feet with virtually every size of rough-cut lumber you are likely to want, in lengths from eight feet (2.44 meters) to twenty feet (6 meters).

Lumber scale, in board feet (BF)

Size	Length (feet)						
	8	10	12	14	16	18	20
(Inches)							
1 x 3	2.0	2.5	3.0	3.5	4.0	4.5	5.0
1 x 4	2.7	3.3	4.0	4.7	5.3	6.0	6.7
1 x 6	4.0	5.0	6.0	7.0	8.0	9.0	10.0
1 x 8	5.3	6.7	8.0	9.3	10.7	12.0	13.3
1 x 10	6.7	8.3	10.0	11.7	13.3	15.0	16.7
1 x 12	8.0	10.0	12.0	14.0	16.0	18.0	20.0
2 x 2	2.7	3.3	4.0	4.7	5.3	6.0	6.7
2 x 4	5.3	6.7	8.0	9.3	10.7	12.0	13.3
2 x 6	8.0	10.0	12.0	14.0	16.0	18.0	20.0
2 x 8	10.7	13.3	16.0	18.7	21.3	24.0	26.7
2 x 10	13.3	16.7	20.0	23.3	26.7	30.0	33.3
2 x 12	16.0	20.0	24.0	28.0	32.0	36.0	40.0
3 x 6	12.0	15.0	18.0	21.0	24.0	27.0	30.0
3 x 8	16.0	20.0	24.0	28.0	32.0	36.0	40.0
3 x 10	20.0	25.0	30.0	35.0	40.0	45.0	50.0
3 x 12	24.0	30.0	36.0	42.0	48.0	54.0	60.0

Size	Length (feet)						
	8	10	12	14	16	18	20
(Inches)							
4 x 4	10.7	13.3	16.0	18.7	21.3	24.0	26.7
4 x 6	16.0	20.0	24.0	28.0	32.0	36.0	40.0
4 x 8	21.3	26.7	32.0	37.3	42.7	48.0	53.3
4 x 10	26.7	33.3	40.0	46.7	53.3	60.0	66.7
4 x 12	32.0	40.0	48.0	56.0	64.0	72.0	80.0
5 x 10	33.3	41.7	50.0	58.3	66.7	75.0	83.3
6 x 6	24.0	30.0	36.0	42.0	48.0	54.0	60.0
6 x 8	32.0	40.0	48.0	56.0	64.0	72.0	80.0
6 x 10	40.0	50.0	60.0	70.0	80.0	90.0	100.0
6 x 12	48.0	60.0	72.0	84.0	96.0	108.0	120.0
8 x 8	42.7	53.3	64.0	74.7	85.3	96.0	106.7
8 x 10	53.3	66.7	80.0	93.3	106.7	120.0	133.3
8 x 12	64.0	80.0	96.0	112.0	128.0	144.0	160.0
10 x 10	66.7	83.3	100.0	116.7	133.3	150.0	166.7
10 x 12	80.0	100.0	120.0	140.0	160.0	180.0	200.0
12 x 12	96.0	120.0	144.0	168.0	192.0	216.0	240.0

already leaning, is to tie a cable to it and pull it down with a piece of heavy equipment, such as a tracked excavator, or a large backhoe, bulldozer, or front-end loader. Yes, a few timbers might be damaged, but this damage will usually occur at the ends of timbers, where mortise and tenon joints are torqued during the pull. With "timber framing for the rest of us," you won't be using those old joints anyway. In effect, you will be just losing some length. You can expect to get a good 12-footer out of an old 14-foot beam, for example.

Dress for the job with tough work clothing, leather or other heavy-duty work gloves, and heavy footwear with thick soles. If working inside a barn, wear a hardhat.

Cultivating Coincidence

On all the buildings I've done with old barn timbers, I would catalog the pieces that I'd been able to procure, using a legal pad or clipboard. I'd record the sectional dimensions of each piece, its useful length, and its condition. Then I would match the cataloged pieces to my plan, to see how I could make the available pieces mesh with what I needed. Sometimes I'd have a few timbers left over — I'd save them for the next project or make them available to another owner-builder — and sometimes I'd have to seek out certain timbers to make up a shortfall. We scored timbers from a variety of sources: eight-by-eights and the like from barns within a 25-mile radius, and lots of good three-by-ten floor joists from the old Masonic hall in West Chazy, New York, as well as from an old Adirondack Inn being torn down for salvage.

I mention these finds to illustrate that it is not just old barns that yield good heavy timbers, but also old commercial buildings and even homes. The best way to increase your chances of finding material like this is to "cultivate your luck." The more tentacles you send out into the world, the better the chances of latching on to something. Some call this networking. I think of it in mathematical terms: There are no coincidences. There is simply a probability of something happening, and the more you do to increase the number of events, the more "coincidences" come through for you. I know all this sounds very "airy-fairy," so here are some practical tips to help you along the way. Believe me, they work.

1. **Consult newspapers and pennysaver-type advertising tabloids**. It is amazing how many farmers and other country folk have timbers — or other valuable building materials — available. In urban areas, Bob advises:

"Read the want ads religiously. The Chicago papers are good for this, but other big-city papers will be, too." Also, you can put a "wanted" ad in yourself. This is a tentacle!

2. **Go to auctions**. But don't just limit yourself to what's being offered. Talk to other people interested in the same stuff. They may know of something they don't need, but which would suit you to a tee. You might lose something at an auction that goes past your price, but score a better deal from someone you meet there.

3. **Talk it up**. Let everyone you meet know that you are looking for old timbers (or cordwood, or straw bales, or windows and doors.) More tentacles.

4. **Keep your eyes peeled while traveling country roads**. Don't be afraid to knock on doors. I do this all the time to procure large stones for megalithic work, and sometimes, when I stop to ask about stones, I discover something else that the people have available. Country people don't usually take good stuff to the dump. They keep it, thinking that they will eventually use it themselves, but, after a couple of years go by, realize that they'll never get around to the project they had in mind and would just as soon let the timbers — or cordwood, or bricks — go to someone who will make good use of the material. Often, someone will say, "I don't have what you're looking for, but old Fred down at the end of the road might be able to help you."

Send out tentacles, and the world will connect with you. Local people would say to us, "I don't see how you get all these good deals. I've been here for twenty years and I never hear of deals like you get." Our secret? We extend ourselves. Go thee and do likewise.

Evaluating Recycled Timbers

Recycled timbers should be carefully evaluated before you buy them or agree to dismantle a building, so carry your wish list (more correctly called a timber schedule) with you to the procurement site. Firstly, timbers have to be of sufficient sectional size and length to do the job. Use actual usable length, allowing for damaged ends or unusable ends due to mortise and tenon joints. Once you've established that you've got something potentially worthwhile, you need to look at each piece carefully for defects that might compromise their use on your project. With barn beams especially, all deterioration is not necessarily obvious: use a sharp knife to poke all four sides to check for soft wood. Reject any soft or "punky" pieces. Sometimes, you might get a good seven-foot post out of a twelve-foot beam, and that's the best you can do. Catalog the piece as a good seven-footer. Do you need ten seven-foot posts? Well, here's one of them.

Fig. 3.1: The author uses a knife to probe an old timber for soft or deteriorated wood. This one was a reject.

Watch out for a mortise carved out of the middle of a timber that you want to use as a girder, as the void will greatly diminish bending strength. However, you might be able to use the piece as a post, or as a girt which will eventually be supported along its length by an intermediate post, or cordwood infilling.

Old timbers that have been under cover are likely to be in good condition, as are those fresh from a demolition site. However, timbers left out in the open for a year or two are almost certain to have begun a process of deterioration. It is so sad to see a beautiful old hand-hewn timber on the ground, and then to turn it over and find an inch of rotted wood on the underside. Even here, though, there is an exception. My friend Bob has some old virgin-growth heartwood timbers — twelve-by-twelves and the like — which have been lying on the ground for years and are still in excellent condition. I saw them myself, and was amazed. They just don't make timbers like these anymore!

The use of recycled timbers may not be allowed in some code enforcement jurisdictions, because the timbers are not "graded" according to the building code — a subject already discussed in Chapter 1. You need to know that you'll be allowed to use the timbers before you spend a lot of time and money on them. As for stress load calculations, it may be hard to even judge the species of a 100-year-old timber, never mind its grade. If we are planning to use the piece as an important girder, it is best to use a conservatively low value as the unit stress rating for both shear and bending. If you see close-grained timbers with small knots or no knots, you know that these timbers are likely to be really strong. They're likely to be really heavy, too.

Timbers from Your Own Land

Some owner-builders may harvest tall straight trees on their own property to make their own timbers for their frame. Hardwoods, in general, are stronger than softwoods, but it's best to compare individual species, as there is considerable overlap in strength characteristics between a list of hardwoods and softwoods. Being generally harder, the hardwoods are more difficult to nail into. You may have to drill holes and use screws to make connections. Also, hardwoods tend to shrink quite a bit more than softwoods. Here are some common woods, beginning with so-called hardwoods — which are actually deciduous or broadleafed trees.

Hardwoods

- **Ash**. Quite strong and usually straight, without a lot of knots. A favorite for baseball bats and hockey sticks. Can develop large checks. The wood is a creamy white.

- **Beech**. Heavy, very strong and quite beautiful. However, beech has a high rate of shrinkage and can suffer from powder post beetles and carpenter ants, so it should be avoided as sill material or as posts. Save it for timbers from the first story upwards. In old timber frame work in the northern hardwood forest — before the current beech blight — beech was often the wood of choice.

- **Birch, White (or Paper)**. Even-grained, medium strength. As a "pioneer species" in the forest, it is not long-lived, so you might have difficulty finding large diameter trees in good condition. Works quite well with hand tools or a chainsaw, when green.

- **Birch, Yellow**. Hard and heavy. Can be stronger than red oak, but can be hard to work. Has a nice wintergreen aroma.

- **Butternut**. Fairly strong for its light weight. The wood is straight-grained and has fairly low shrinkage for a hardwood.

- **Cherry, Black**. Rot-resistant and strong. In some parts of the northeast, it is fairly common. Black cherry is a pretty wood, but, if you have it, you may want to reserve it for furniture, cabinets, or special detailing, to make boards instead of beams.

- **Hickory**. Probably the strongest of North American woods. I use shagbark hickory for levers when I do megalithic stone work. It shrinks a lot. Mill it fairly soon after cutting to reduce splitting.

- **Locust, Black**. Very strong and heavy. The only truly decay-resistant hardwood, although this should not be a big issue, unless you want to build a pole-barn building without using pressure-treated posts. Exceptional for sills or where constant weathering can be expected. Can be very difficult to work.

- **Maple, Red and Sugar**. Straight and non-spiral growth trees are suitable for timber framing if worked green. If the tree grows in a spiral, as it sometimes does, expect twisting in the timbers. Quite a lot of shrinkage can be expected and rot resistance is poor.

- **Oak, Red**. Moderate shrinkage, strong, works well. Not as decay resistant as the white oak, so keep it off of the sills. Has an attractive grain.

- **Oak, White**. The classic hardwood for timber framing, white oak is strong, durable, and decay resistant. It shrinks a lot, but in exposed rafters, joists, and girders, shrinkage is not really a problem. Sobon and Schroeder (1984) say it is very workable for traditional timber framing, but ten years later, Sobon (1994) says it is "more difficult to work than red oak or beech." My personal experience is limited to making a few chainsaw cuts to join a ten-by-twelve white oak girder over a couple of eight-by-eight white oak posts. This is not a problem when the timbers are still fairly young. Once hardwoods are fully seasoned, sparks will fly off your chain!

Softwoods

- **Balsam Fir**. Looks like spruce, but not as strong. Very pitchy. Balsam firs snap off like toothpicks on our property during windstorms, so I presently have a low opinion of them. Still, if you choose the timbers carefully and have the stress load calculations checked over, balsam fir can do the job.

- **Cedar, Northern White**. This is one of my favorites for both log-ends and as timber frame material here in Northern New York. It is plentiful and inexpensive, very easy to cut and work, and plenty strong enough for the heavy-framing applications I use it for: posts, sills, and plates. I don't use it for joists, rafters, and unsupported girders, as white pine is stronger and is also plentiful. White cedar has a pleasant aroma, without being overwhelming.

- **Cedar, Red**. Very rot resistant, so a good choice for sills and exposed applications. It may be hard to find trees large enough to get a quantity of heavy timbers. Great for unmilled (round) porch posts. And aromatic.

- **Hemlock, Eastern**. Heavy when green. While strong on bending, hemlock is not very strong on shear. If using hemlock for girders, be sure to have the stress load calculations double-checked for shear. Watch out for "shake," the term for separations between annual growth rings. This is, I suspect, where the low shear strength originates. Great for posts — and any timber frame needs a lot of these — but watch out for splinters. There is something particularly painful about hemlock slivers. Sobon (1994) says, "I often relegate it to areas where hands won't touch it."

- **Pine, Eastern White**. Soft and lightweight, yet plenty strong for most timber-framing applications. A pleasure to work with. White pine was popular amongst the colonists for all building purposes. Outer layers can be quite sappy. If so, you may have to dry the milled timbers in the sun a couple of weeks before handling, a good idea in any case.

- **Pine, Red or Norway**. Similar strength characteristics as white pine, but in my experience at Earthwood, the red pine twists a lot more than the white, and for this reason I now go with the white if given a choice. My local sawyer agrees. Therefore, as joists or rafters, be sure to block red pine members at each end to prevent twisting. Of course, this is always good building practice.

• **Spruce, Eastern**. Sobon and Schroeder (1984) say, "It is a good choice for timber frames because of its straightness, small knots, light weight, strength, and resistance to splitting." Good recommendation. My personal experience with spruce is limited to using it as tongue-in-groove flooring and as log-ends in a cordwood wall, where it has served very well for both purposes.

• **Tamarack (Eastern Larch)**. Another log-end favorite, but I have no personal experience with tamarack (also called larch) in timber framing. Sobon (1984) says it is "A strong wood with small knots, it grows straight, is resistant to decay, and has medium shrinkage." As with red cedar, it may be a problem finding trees large enough.

Timber from Small Sawmills

The wood descriptions above are general in nature. A particular species can exhibit varying characteristics depending on where it grows. A local sawyer's advice is as valuable as the list above, particularly one who has many years of experience in the area.

Local sawyers charge for their lumber by the board foot. Logically, you would think that you'd get a break on price for an eight-by-eight over, say, four two-by-eights or eight one-by-eights of the same length. After all, the board footage is the same in all cases, and the sawyer has far fewer cuts to make with an eight-by-eight. You should get a price break, right? Well, I've never seen that happen. You pay by the board foot, end of story. The only exception is that if you give your sawyer your complete timber schedule and ask him (or her, though I have yet to meet a female sawyer) to give you a cost for the whole job, the generic "he" will take things like this into consideration, especially if there are other mills in the area.

If possible, leave your timber schedule with at least three local sawmills for pricing. But also ask about how long it will take to finish the order and whether or not they can arrange for delivery. Most sawyers are too busy to deliver on their

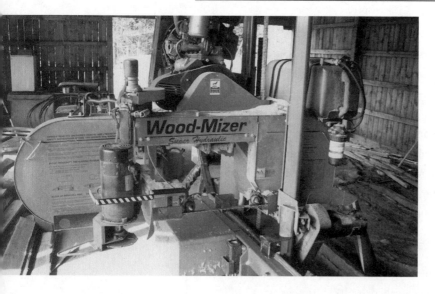

Fig. 3.2: A sawyer in West Chazy, New York, tows this portable Wood Mizer bandsaw mill to private woodlots to make lumber.

own, but they often know someone with a truck who can deliver the timbers to you. You can also use your own pickup truck if you are not too far from the sawmill. Several loads will be required, and fresh-cut timbers are well, heavy. Length of timber is limited to around ten feet for pick-up transport, unless the truck is equipped with an overhead wood rack. I hauled all the timbers for our new addition at Earthwood (Chapter 5) in our Nissan pick-up, but it took a few loads, at 18 miles round trip.

All sawyers think — or say — that they are accurate, and most are, but take a tape measure with you and quietly check out a few timbers that are already lying around. I work with two local sawyers. "Sawyer 1" has a bandsaw and "Sawyer 2" has a traditional large circular saw. Each one makes very regular dimensional timbers — I have never had a complaint about this — but Sawyer 1 sometimes lets some shoddy pieces go through: excessive wain, heart rot, large knots on the edge of the timber creating a weakness. The other guy doesn't let this type of thing pass.

I usually end up going with Sawyer 2, even though he is a little more expensive, because of timber quality and the fact that he is reliable in having the job ready when he says it will be. Also, he will give me special attention for some of the personal quirky projects that we have going at Earthwood. Once, I needed a couple of six-by-eight posts resawn on an angle along their length. I showed up with the timbers, and he stopped production to accommodate me, and did a good job. Another time, he pulled five very cylindrical logs out of his pile for use as rollers at one of our megalithic stone workshops. This kind of service is beyond price.

Portable Sawmills

Jim, my next-door neighbor, recently built a major addition to his house, using the kinds of timber-framing methods described in this book. He hired a local fellow with a portable bandsaw mill to come up and cut all of the timbers from logs that Jim had hauled out of his own woods. The timbers were cut straight and were of good regular dimensions.

Some of these portable mill operators charge by the hour, some by the board foot, some will do it either way. With heavy timbers, you are probably better off paying by the hour. This is what Jim did, and what he advises. He paid $35 an hour and all the heavy timbers and boards for his addition were cut in about six hours; his addition is fourteen by twenty-four feet, two stories. A lot of the wood was ash, a genuine hardwood, but this did not present a problem for the sawyer. Jim and a friend helped by rolling the logs onto the machine. He reckons that all of the timbers and lumber for a house could be done in a couple of days for about $500, once the logs have been dragged out of the woods and gathered together where the sawmill is set up.

With lots of small boards and two-by-eights, paying by the board foot might work out just as well or better. Look sawyers up in the Yellow Pages under "Sawmills." Call and ask their rates (by the hour and by the board foot), and whether or not there is a travel or set-up charge.

If you are blessed with having straight timbers of sufficient size on your property, hiring a portable sawmill is one of the most economical ways to obtain quality timbers. These portable bandsaws, such as Wood-Mizer and others, can make high quality timbers providing, of course, that the operator is experienced.

Chainsaw Mills

There is an alternative timber procurement strategy for those with their own stand of large straight trees, and that is to make the timbers yourself with a chainsaw mill, essentially an attachment for a chainsaw. There are several different styles and qualities and costs vary a great deal. Here are some choices, with contact information for all of them found in Appendix C. See also the Sidebar on pages 54–55.

- **The Beam Machine**. First, you nail a two-by-four to the log that you want to make into a beam. The Beam Machine is an inexpensive ($40) bar attachment that slides along the two-by-four. Their ad says the "dog-tooth pivoting action takes most of the strain out of sawing because it supports the weight of the saw and provides you with a smooth, leveraged sawing motion."

- **The Granberg Mini-Mill**. Similar to the Beam Machine, except that it comes with a 12-foot metal guide rail to fasten to a two-by-six plank (not provided), and an extra handle and guide assembly to help pull the vertically-mounted chainsaw along the rail. About $80.

Comparing Two Chainsaw Milling Guides

Before commenting on the inexpensive chainsaw milling guides, I figured I'd better test them. Friends Bruce Kilgore and Doug Kerr, both of whom play a part in Chapter 5, were interested in helping to conduct the test. I already had a Beam Machine (www.beammachine. com) and Bruce had recently purchased a Haddon Lumbermaker (www.haddontools.com). On the advice of Ted Mather, the inventor of my Beam Machine, I used an ordinary crosscut chain, not the special ripping chain recommended by most other chainsaw mill manufacturers. The regular chain, Mather says, gives a much smoother cut.

Granberg International, whose $80 Mini-Mill is quite similar to the Lumbermaker says on their website: "Your regular stock chain on your saw works okay when it is sharpened correctly. All top angles must be the same uniform angle (25, 30, 35˚) and your depth gauges must be at the same height, no more than thirty-five thousandths inch below the cutting edge of the tooth. For better ripping results, resharpen your stock chain to a 0˚ top plate angle from the 25, 30, or 35˚ angle mentioned before. The 0˚ top plate angle reduces the power needed to rip and produces smoother lumber than regular stock chain." However, Granberg also states that ordinary chain, even with specialty sharpening, does not work as well as their own Granberg Ripping Chain.

Bruce and I did not have any ripping chain and conducted our test with a machine-sharpened crosscut saw — regular crosscut sharpening — as per Mather's advice. Our test logs were balsam fir, about 12 inches in diameter and eight feet in length. First, we tried the Beam Machine, which requires that an ordinary

(finished) two-by-four be screwed along the length of the log as a guide for the first cut. We propped the log up on a couple of shorter logs so that the tip of the 18-inch bar on my Stihl 029 chainsaw was well clear of the ground.

The Beam Machine is simply a 12-inch-long (30.5 centimeter) piece of channel iron welded to a pivoting mechanism which clamps onto the chainsaw's bar with two strong setscrews. The channel iron fits neatly to the two-by-four that has been fastened along the log's length. The mechanism allows the operator to import a vertical and straight cut as the unit is slid along the two-by-four guide track. All three of us tried the Beam Machine, and we found that we could rip the first slab off the edge of the log in about three minutes. We also tried Bruce's saw, but it was not sharpened as well, and took considerably longer, pointing out the importance of a well-sharpened chain. We were all impressed with the smoothness of the cut using a regular chain.

After the first slab was cut away, we had a nice flat surface for remounting the two-by-four guide. Always, the Beam Machine must travel along the guide. We simply rotated the log by 90 degrees, so that we could work vertically once again on the adjacent (second) cut. We marked the small end of the log with a pencil, showing the square eight-by-eight cross-section of the beam that we wanted to make. Just before beginning a cut, we would barely tickle the end of the log with the saw to find out if we would, indeed, be cutting on the correct — outside — side of our line. On the second cut, I failed to keep the metal guide firmly on the two-by-four track and the saw came out of the other end of the log almost an inch out of plumb.

On this first test log, we also tried Bruce's Haddon Lumbermaker, which operated on the same principle, but used a two-by-six guide instead of a two-by-four. Combined with a superior bearing for a pivot mechanism, we found the Haddon on its wider track was easier to keep on a straight vertical line. As we used the same saw, there was no difference in the time it took to make a cut.

In four cuts, we had a passable eight-by-eight post or beam, except that — thanks to my inexperience on the second cut — the last three feet of one end took a decided turn, so the cross section of that end is an inch out of square. Well, it would do as a post!

We made a nearly perfect eight-by-nine beam out of the next log, again using both machines. All dimensions were within a quarter-inch. Again, the $85 Haddon was easier to control than the $40 Beam Machine. In fairness, I think that with practice, an operator can do an adequate job with the less expensive tool, but if I were cutting a number of heavy timbers for a job, I'd say it's probably worth the extra money for the Haddon. Doug and Bruce concurred. All told, with experience, a sharp chain, and an adequately powerful saw, an eight- to ten-foot heavy timber should be possible to make every half hour with either of these simple chainsaw attachments.

Fig. 3.3a: The Haddon Lumbermaker uses a wide two-by-six trackway for improved stability.

Fig. 3.3b: Doug Kerr cuts a slab off a fir log with the Beam Machine.

• **Alaskan Small Log Mill**. This is the smallest of the Alaskan series of chainsaw mills, "perfect for the homeowner, woodworker or carpenter who owns a 3.8 cubic inch saw with a 20-inch bar," according to the manufacturer. The Alaskan mills employ a different sort of guide from the Beam Machine or the Mini-Mill. The saw runs horizontally along the log, not vertically. The first cut is made using a plank guide, and additional cuts run along the first cut. About $120 in 2003.

• **Basic Alaskan Mill**. These mills range from the 24-inch Alaskan Mill, which will make a 20-inch (51 centimeter) cut ($150), all the way to the big 56-inch Alaskan Mill which will cut a 54-inch (137 centimeter) swath through the log ($220), although I can't imagine why you would need any more than the 20-inch cut for making heavy timbers. None of the prices, of course, include the saw, special bar, or the special chainsaw milling chain, also called a "ripping chain." It is not recommended to try to run any Alaskan Mill with a saw of less than 3.8 cubic inches of displacement, and larger is better.

• **Complete Alaskan Mills**. These are big, heavy-duty items and will allow you to cut wide thick slabs easily. You can hook up two chainsaw power heads to one bar and chain, which more than doubles the effective power. These mills run from $470 to $600, and the chainsaws, bars, and chains would add a great deal to these figures.

• **Logosol Timber Jig**. My editor for this book, Richard Freudenberger, tested this chainsaw attachment, similar to the Basic Alaskan Mills, and wrote a comprehensive report for *BackHome* magazine's September/ October, 2003 issue. In the article, Richard says, "At 5½ pounds, the Timber Jig is light enough to be carried into the woods with the saw. Yet if you wanted to set up a permanent work site to cut timbers or planks for a building project, it would be a simple matter to make a timber log table to support your logs at a comfortable working height." Using an aged Husqvarna saw with a displacement of about five cubic inches, and a narrow-kerf ripping chain supplied by Logosol, Richard was able to cut through white pine at a rate of about 3.2 feet per minute. Richard concludes, "For the hobby wood-cutter, the Timber Jig is a $155 investment that will probably pay for itself in short order. In touting the tool as an economy lumber maker, the manufacturer may be hiding the fact that it's actually an excellent timber maker as well. Even limited by its 8½-inch (21.6 centimeter) depth, ripping out your own eight-by-twelve beams for a timber-frame project would save a bundle over buying them." Richard's complete article, with details of how to use the Timber Jig, is available in *BackHome* back issue No. 66. Write BackHome Back Issues, P.O. Box 70, Hendersonville, NC 28793, call: (800) 992•2546 or log on to: www.BackHomeMagazine.com.

Fig. 3.4: Richard Freudenberger tests the Logosol Timber Jig portable chainsaw mini-mill. Photo by Don Osby, reproduced by permission of BackHome Magazine, No. 66, p. 48.

Both the Logosol and the various Alaskan Mills are a step up from the simple chainsaw guides like the Beam Machine and the Granberg Mini-Mill, and are recommended for larger projects. Yet another step up, and reflected in the cost, is the …

- **Better Built Ripsaw by SIR Incorporated**. This mill is also driven by a chainsaw head, but the bar and chain are replaced with a mounted bandsaw mill. In an article in *Independent Sawmill and Woodlot Management* magazine (August/ September, 2003), author Dave Boyt speaks well of this "simple and economical chainsaw-powered bandmill." Although very much less expensive than full-sized portable sawmills, the $1,589 cost — plus the chainsaw — may not justify itself in a single project. However, it might be a very good investment for someone who anticipates additional homesteading projects in the future, or simply wants to add value to trees on the woodlot which need to be thinned.

An excellent source for purchasing many of these mills is Bailey's, a woodsman's supply house. Much of the information above comes from their 2003 Master Catalog. See Appendix C: Resources.

Making your own lumber with a chainsaw mill or bar guide is hard work, and great care must be taken both for safety and to maintain an acceptable standard of quality. Still, with a little practice, even the simplest guide attachments will yield good and useful heavy timbers.

Making timbers with a chainsaw presupposes that you are handy in the woods with the tool, as the first task will be felling the trees and maneuvering them to a clearing where you can work on the trunks. If you are not already an experienced woodsman, have someone who is teach you how to operate the saw safely and how to take down trees. Even better, take a chainsaw operation and safety course, as I should have done. I learned from experience and by necessity, but once, after about ten years of experience, I cut through a log and the tip of the saw kicked back on some hard object below. The bar, with the chain still moving, kicked back and bounced off my nose. It took a skilled plastic surgeon to make me into the good-looking guy I am today.

This book will not attempt to teach chainsaw skills. There are books and articles that do — you can search the internet — but a certified course is better. I will say that you should always wear safety chaps to protect your legs and body, and safety helmets for eye, ear and head protection. My son and I share a set of chaps, and, yes, they have been grazed on occasion. The reality is that chainsaws, handled incorrectly, can maim or kill, and so they must be treated with respect and vigilant concentration.

Having said all that, people comfortable with a chainsaw and not afraid of work can use these chainsaw mills to provide all the lumber they need, if they've got the trees. In a wooded building site, just clearing the house site itself, and a driveway to it, will often yield enough material to build a house. Just be careful out there!

Seasoning the Timbers

How long to air-dry or season the timbers before use is a much-debated question. The best answer I have encountered is from contemporary timber framer and colleague Steve Chappell in his book *A Timber Framer's Workshop*, listed in the Bibliography. Steve uses the term "curing" to describe the early stages of the seasoning process. He describes this initial phase:

Once the tree dies and is milled, the wood fibers begin to relax and take on their natural shape. There is usually an immediate reaction to being milled in the form of crowning, warping, or twisting, resulting from the inherent tension in the wood, but no shrinkage will occur until all of the free water (moisture in the cell cavities), and the bound water (moisture in the cell walls) begins to leave. (Chappell, 1998, p. 139)

Chappell says that 90 percent of these deformations due to natural stresses being relaxed will take place in the first six months, but adds that "the first eight to twelve weeks is the most rapid curing stage" and that "it is during these early stages that the most dramatic changes will take place." (Chappell, pp. 139–140)

My own experience with the new heavy timbers we used for our new Earthwood addition (Chapter 5) bears this out. I paid a little more for early delivery of the timbers, and the heaviest ones managed to get ten to twelve weeks of excellent drying conditions, a big plus. The white pine timbers were lighter to handle, kept their straightness, and shrunk only marginally on their breadth and width.

I used to think — I suppose I read it somewhere — that the old-time timber merchants would store wood for years to supply builders with dry timbers. Chappell says otherwise, that builders were "more concerned with properly curing their timbers and allowing them to season *for as long as was practicable*." Emphasis mine.

To minimize twisting and other seasoning defects, get your timbers home from the sawmill as soon as possible after they are cut, and stack them in good parallel courses, with one-inch wooden stickers between the courses. Choose a flat, well-drained site without vegetation. (Mow the grass as needed.) If the timbers are already showing signs of mold when you get them to your site, you should lay them out individually in the sun for a few days to kill the fungus.

Wood rot, incidentally, is caused by fungi, which use the cellulose in wood as a food. But fungi also need a constant damp condition. If moisture content in wood is below about 18 percent, the fungi will not flourish, although the spores might remain alive, just waiting for more favorable times. This is why proper stacking of wood is so dependent on good ventilation, which is an excellent preventative to rot. This is also why exposed beams in a building are so resistant to fungi and rot: they enjoy superb ventilation. But back to the stacking.

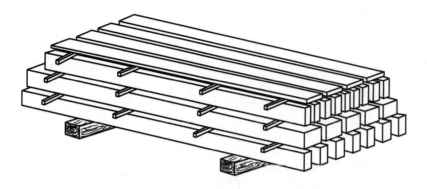

Fig. 3.5: The timbers for the Earthwood sunroom were stacked with the five-by-ten rafters at the bottom, the eight-inch-wide posts and girders next, then the four-by-eight floor joists, and finally some two-by-eights at the top. Two railway ties were used to get the stack a few inches off of the ground. Stickers were made from scrap pieces of one-by wood given to me by the sawyer.

Have a good quantity of dry stickers, which are lengths of regularly-dimensioned scrap wood, to place laterally between courses. They should be at least an inch thick to prevent mold, and at least three stickers should be used per course of wood with timbers up to ten feet long, and four or more with longer timbers. Each course in the stack should be made with timbers of the same vertical dimension. A tall stack is preferable to a wide stack, because the extra weight of the wood acts as a clamp to help minimize any twisting of the wood during the curing process. And put the timbers that you are going to use first on the top of the pile, not the bottom!

"Sticker burn" or discoloration can occur where the stickers are placed. If you care about this, get a friend to help you restack the pile, top to bottom, twice during the curing, which, again, puts the first needed timbers on top. Move the stickers a few inches so as not to exacerbate the sticker burn. If you are planning on sanding all the timbers anyway, sticker burn is of less consequence.

I conclude this chapter with a picture of the way I stacked my timbers for our Earthwood sunroom project.

CHAPTER 4

Building Techniques:
Timber Framing for the Rest of Us

To this point, we have spoken of considerations appropriate for all timber framing projects. But now we have reached a juncture where traditional timber framers go one way and the rest of us take another path. As Yogi Berra said at a college commencement speech, "When you get to that fork in the road take it." I say, "Let's start at the bottom and work up."

Foundation Options

Timber framing can be married quite happily to a variety of foundation methods, which, in general, can be characterized under four separate categories: piers, footings, masonry walls, and slab-on-grade.

1. **Piers**. Piers can also be called pillars, columns or posts, and can be made of wood (such as 75-year ground contact six-by-six timbers or railway ties) or of poured concrete. Concrete piers can be in the form of truncated pyramids, such as my friend Steve Sugar did near Hilo, Hawaii (Fig. 4.1 on page 62 and Fig. 4.18 on page 77) or they can be poured within heavy cardboard tubes called Sona tubes. Whether the piers are wood or concrete, they should extend down to below the code-specified frost line where you are building. In northern New York, this is considered to be four feet. It is also a good idea to distribute the load of the post or pier on a large flat stone, say 12 to 16 inches (30.5 to 40.6 centimeters) square. The top of the pillar should be six to twelve inches (15.2 to 30.5 centimeters) clear of grade to protect any wooden post above it, or the sill plate, from damp. Reinforced concrete columns made with Sona tubes can extend three or four feet above grade, if you want to make use of the crawl space under the building.

Fig. 4.1: Steve and Eileen Sugar's home near Hilo, Hawaii, is built above grade on about twenty of these concrete pillars. The pressure treated posts are tied down to the pillar with mechanical fasteners made for the purpose. You'll see the house later, in Fig. 4.18, and the fasteners in Fig. 4.17.

While I have nothing against piers made with Sona tubes, my personal view is that the 75-year pressure-treated piers will probably last just as long, are cheaper and easier to install by the inexperienced owner-builder, and if it comes to it, easier to replace.

2. **Footings**. Generally made of poured concrete, footings might typically be 12 to 16 inches wide and at least 8 inches (203 millimeters) thick.

With small buildings, such as a sauna or our little guesthouses, I "float" the footings on a good pad of percolating material. See slab-on-grade below. I call this foundation a "floating ring beam" and its construction is detailed in both my books *Complete Book of Cordwood Masonry Housebuilding* and *The Sauna* (see Bibliography). (Fig. 4.2.)

With most northern construction today, the footings are installed below frost line, whether an earth-sheltered space is desired below grade, or simply a "crawl space." This leads us to:

Fig. 4.2: La Casita, a small guesthouse at Earthwood, has its simple post and beam frame founded on a "floating ring beam." See also Fig. 2.21.

3. **Masonry walls**. Supported by either footings or the slab-on-grade, masonry walls can be poured concrete, block or even stone masonry. These walls can be of the desired height according to the house style (basement, crawl space, etc.) and should be at least as wide as the post and beam frame

and any intended infilling. For example, if the builder wants a 16-inch-wide cordwood wall, built within a strong post-and-beam frame, the supporting wall (and footings) should also be 16 inches wide. (Fig. 4.3.)

Fig. 4.3: Here, the posts — and the cordwood walls — are built up on a pressure-treated wooden plate one course of blocks higher than the floating slab.

4. **Slab-on-grade.** This is also known as the "floating slab" or the "Alaskan slab." It works on the sound principal that frost heaving is caused by water freezing and expanding below the building. The two approaches taken to avoid this problem are (1) to go down below maximum frost depth with the footings or (2) to prevent water from collecting under the foundation in the first place. The second approach is the way the slab-on-grade works. The poured concrete slab "floats" on a pad of percolating material such as coarse sand, gravel, or crushed stone. The pad drains any water to a place further down grade. There is no water under the foundation to freeze, so no nasty uplifting expansion (called "heaving") takes place. Again, see *Complete Book of Cordwood Masonry Housebuilding* for a thorough discussion. But, be sure to follow local code, too. The slab-on-grade does appear in the new International Building Code, now used in most states.

Incidentally, Frank Lloyd Wright liked both the floating slab and another foundation method, which works on a similar principle, called the rubble trench. By this method, a trench is dug down to just below frost level, and then filled with fairly coarse (potato-sized) stone. Footings are formed and poured on this stone at grade level. The trench is drained to some point down grade, so the method is best suited for a site with sufficient grade differential.

The best discussion of the rubble trench foundation, good enough to build from, appears in the excellent book *Foundations and Concrete Work* (see Bibliography). Using just the information in that book, Ki Light made his rubble trench foundation. A concrete footing floats on the packed rubble, and his post and beam frame (and his straw bales) are founded on this footing. You've already seen Ki's house in Fig. 1.2.

The present book, though, is about timber framing, not foundation methods. Maybe someday I'll do a book called *Foundations for the Rest of Us*, but don't hold your breath. Almost any good generalized building book (including *Foundations and Concrete Work*, page 17) will show you how to set up "batter boards" to establish a square foundation. This fine inexpensive book also explains the slab-on-grade and other foundation methods.

Post Height

Post height should be figured at the planning stage and your plans should include an elevation view of each side of the house, including any gables. This view will show the posts, the heavy timber girt above them (also called the girding beam) and floor joists, if supported from below by the girt. (The alternative is to hang the floor joists on the girt with metal joist hangers made for the purpose.)

If you are building your own house, chances are that you will be designing it yourself as well. Post height can be figured by working back from the desired ceiling height. For example, let's say that the plan calls for the ceiling joists to hang from the girts with joist hangers, and, further, that the joists are the same depth as the girts, perhaps ten inches. If you want to maintain eight feet to the underside of the ceiling (or exposed floor joists), then the posts will be the same height as the ceiling or underside of exposed joists. If the joists are installed directly above the girts, then you can shorten the posts by the thickness of the girt and still maintain the desired headroom. With an eight-inch thick girt, for example, a seven-foot four-inch post will still give eight feet of headroom to the underside of the joists.

Another way I have figured this, at four different houses now, is to base everything on the doorframe. Let's say we start with a standard six-foot eight-inch (203 centimeter) door and use an eight-inch-thick girt as the top part of the doorframe. (Six-foot eight inches plus eight inches equals seven-foot four inches, or 224 centimeters.) Further, let's say that we support the ceiling joists on top of the girt, not with joist hangers. In this example, headroom clearance will be seven foot four inches to the underside of the joists. With exposed eight-inch joists, the visual effect is eight feet (244 centimeters) to the ceiling planks, quite sufficient unless you are very tall. This is the way it is downstairs at Earthwood as well as in the new solar room upstairs (see next chapter) and we like it. The main upstairs area slopes up from about eight feet at the edges to about nine feet at the center.

All of this is a matter of individual taste, but have such details well planned before you order materials.

Fastening the Timber Frame to the Foundation

Whatever foundation method is selected, local codes will vary on their requirements for tying the timber frame down to it, depending on the likelihood of hurricanes, tornadoes and earthquakes. In most areas, a heavy timber frame will not vertically leap off of the foundation so the main consideration is to prevent the sill plate or the posts from moving laterally. This is most easily accomplished by joining the posts to the foundation with positioning pins. As northern New York does not suffer from any of the aforementioned natural disasters, this is what I have been doing with all our buildings since 1975.

The joint between posts and foundation. Sometimes just the posts are fastened to the foundation, and infilling (such as cob, cordwood, or straw bale) completes the wall between posts after the frame is completed, such as La Casita in Fig. 4.2. Our downstairs doorposts at Earthwood are also pinned directly to the foundation. I pour the footings or the floating slab without placing positioning pins (anchor bolts) in the concrete, for two reasons: 1) It is difficult to trowel the concrete smoothly within a few inches of the anchor bolt, leaving an irregular bearing surface for the post to stand upon and 2) Murphy's Law tells you that the pin or anchor bolt will not be in the right place when you come to use it, particularly with doorframes.

Therefore, I install my positioning pins in another way. After the concrete has set — it is hard and strong after two weeks — I use a carbide masonry bit to drill holes into the concrete exactly where they should be. I can measure off the corners and double-check my measurements. These holes are drilled the same depth as the length of the expansion shield which will be later driven into them. These cylindrical shields, available at any building supply store, are made of lead and are split in half to receive a certain size lag screw. The shield has all the pertinent information molded right into the lead. For example, you might see "⅝D, ⅜S" embossed in the lead. This tells you to drill the hole with a five-eighths-inch (1.6 centimeter) Drill bit, and that you will insert a three-eighths-inch (1.0 centimeter) screw into the shield later. Drill the hole a smidgen deeper than the length of the shield. I find two-inch (5.0 centimeter) shields to be convenient: not too much drilling, but plenty strong enough. Blow the dust out of the hole with a straw, but wear eye and nose protection.

The shields are driven into the clean hole with a hammer so that the top of the shield is flush with the concrete surface. Next, turn the hex-headed lag screw into the shield with a socket wrench until the screw is tight. Choose a length so that when the hex head is cut off (takes 30 seconds with a hacksaw), about two inches will be left exposed above the concrete. If you use a two-inch shield, then, you will want to buy four-inch lag screws.

There is another fastener that will do this job a little more easily and has the advantage of leaving a threaded end proud of the foundation, for the installation of angle iron as a fastening aid or for the installation of sill plates (described below.) Simpson's fastener of this kind is called an "Easy-Set pin drive expansion anchor," quite a mouthful, so just ask the clerk for an expansion anchor or strike bolt. A pin sticks out of the anchor, and when the pin is struck, the anchor expands tightly into the hole. So, again, drill a hole (Simpson recommends a hole one-sixteenths-inch greater than the anchor diameter), insert the anchor, and give the pin a good blow with a hammer. Choose a length of strike bolt appropriate for the application. For most purposes, leave the top of the anchor's shaft extending two inches proud of the foundation. The downside of strike bolts is that they are about three times as expensive as the expansion shield method, so I still use the shields and lag screws. They don't call me Rob Roy for nothing.

Now, before installing the post, there is a very important step which must not be omitted. Cut a square of material — called, by the Brits, a "damp-proof course"— the same size as the footprint of the post. An eight-by-eight post requires an eight-inch by eight-inch (20 by 20 centimeter) square of damp-proof material. I have used pieces of asphalt shingle as well as 240-pound roll roofing for the purpose, both successfully. These materials are almost an eighth of an inch thick. Before placing the posts, position the square of asphalt over the anchor pin and press down. Sometimes you can actually press the square down over the pin right to the foundation. Sometimes, you may have to make an impression and actually cut the little hole out with a knife. In either case, you will now have the post's footprint completely covered to prevent "rising damp." This protects the underside of the post from deterioration by damp and rot. Believe me, it works. I have done this for 25 years with no deterioration in any post or doorframe. (The International Residential Code at Section R323 also requires "an impervious moisture barrier," wherever a wooden post meets concrete.) I have seen others put the post directly on the concrete without the square of asphalt damp proofing, and those posts have deteriorated badly. Plus, the almost eighth-inch thick piece acts as a steadying or leveling influence when it comes to actually standing the post in place.

Erecting an individual post is a two-person, two-step process, because of the positioning pin. First, the post is stood up onto the pin. Concrete blocks can be used as positioning aids so that you know that the post will stand on just the right footprints, as seen in Figs. 4.4 and 4.5. Make sure that the post is the right length and has two good squared ends. Now, while one person holds the post, the other person, on a stepladder, gives it one stiff "thwack" with a heavy hammer, making an imprint on the underside of the post. Next, the post is taken down and a hole of the same diameter as the threaded lag screw is drilled at least as deep as the pin is high, say two inches in our example. Finally, the post is stood up again, but this time it is there to stay, the pin in the hole keeping it in the right place, even during an earthquake.

By the one-post-at-a-time method, each post must be supported in two different directions by long diagonal scrap timbers, nailed to wooden stakes pounded firmly into the ground. (If the post is in the middle of a slab, or at some intermediate point along the wall, horizontal pieces of flat scrap, such as two-foot long (61 centimeter) pieces of two-by-four, can be screwed to the bottom of the post to act as stabilizers. A piece of plywood in the shape of an isosceles triangle will work nicely, too. Review figure 2.21).

Fig. 4.4: The damp-proof square covers the footprint where the eight-by-eight posts will stand.

Fig. 4.5: Guided by adjacent blocks, Rohan holds the post in position over the pin. When Rohan nodded his head, I hit it with a sledgehammer. (The post, that is.)

Sill Plates and Sill Beams

Very often, a two-inch thick sill plate is fastened to the foundation, and the wooden frame is attached to that. This sill plate is usually bolted to the foundation all around its perimeter. Yet another neighbor, Chris Ryan — we live in a community of owner-builders — did this at his new garage. First, he laid a course of ordinary eight-inch concrete blocks around the perimeter of his slab, except where his doors would be, because he wanted to keep his posts (and his cordwood masonry) about eight inches (20 centimeters) off the slab. (Fig. 4.3 is actually a detail from the Ryan garage.) Then, at appropriate locations, he filled block cores with concrete and placed anchor bolts into the fresh mix. (Use any bagged dry concrete mix for this, such as Sakrete® or equivalent.) Anchor bolts are in the shape of a long upper-case letter L, and come in various sizes, but a typical one for this purpose would be eight inches long and one-half-inch in diameter, with the top few inches threaded to receive hex-headed nuts. Chris left the bolts sticking out about 1½ inches (3.8 centimeters) proud of the top of the blocks.

For an eight- or ten-foot sill plate, place an anchor bolt such that there will be one about six inches (152 millimeters) in from each end, and one in the middle of the plank's length. Although PT material will not deteriorate in this application, it is still a good ideal to install a roll of Sill Seal® or equivalent. Sill Seal is a blue foam that comes in a roll, eight inches wide and about one-quarter-inch thick. It will help resist rising damp and will also seal against drafts coming in where the sill plate meets the foundation.

Set the plates on top of the anchor bolts and hit the plate with a hammer at each bolt location to make a mark. Drill a five-eighths-inch (1.6 centimeter) hole through the plate at each mark, and install the plate using flat washers and half-inch nuts. Chris countersunk the holes in the plate to accommodate the washers and nuts, but with most infillings, a nut and bolt assembly protruding a half inch proud of the plate will not present a problem.

On a poured footing or slab, you may wish to place the anchor bolts right in the fresh concrete, but be sure to get them in useful positions. If you do make an error, you can always hacksaw any errant bolts off, and install pins by the expansion shield or strike bolt methods already described.

With traditional timber framing, the sill might be a heavy timber, such as an eight-by-eight or better. Timber framer Steve Chappell tells me that these heavy sills are normally installed first, and the bents are raised up on them, with the mortises and tenons all ready to join each other at the time of raising. Where wind uplift is not a code issue, Steve simply pins these heavy timbers to the foundation. He uses metal foundation straps where required by code. You can jump ahead to Fig. 4.54 to see these straps used in an area prone to earthquakes. Steve feels strongly, as I do, that heavy timber frames have a powerful natural resistance against wind uplift.

Most of "the rest of us" place posts directly down on the foundation (not forgetting the damp-proof course) or use a two-by sill plate, like Chris did at his garage. However, at Log End Cottage, our first timber frame structure, built in 1975, we used heavy ten-by-ten (25.4 by 25.4 centimeter) barn beam sills at the gable ends and full-sized three-by-ten sills along the longer sidewalls. The three-by-tens were fastened to the top of the block wall by the method described for Chris's garage. With the ten-by-tens, we simply set anchor bolts sticking out two inches, made an impression on the underside of the sill with a good strike of the hammer, drilled the receiving holes, and placed the sill beams onto the foundation over the 1970s equivalent of Sill Seal. This stopped the sill from moving laterally. There is no way that this heavy sill and building is going to leap upward off of the positioning pins.

If code requires that you anchor such heavy timbers down, you will need to use threaded rod set in grouted block cores or into the poured concrete footings. The rod would have to extend eleven inches (28.0 centimeters) for a ten-by-ten (or ten inches if you want to countersink the washer and nut.) Alternatively, you may be able to fasten the girder by other strap fasteners set in the concrete for the purpose — see Joe Zinni's case study at the end of the chapter — or you might choose the angle iron method, described next.

The angle iron method can be very useful where a doorframe is installed after the rest of the frame is already built. However, you can use the technique in all sorts of applications, so I will spend a little time on it now.

Any good building supply will have galvanized angle iron of various sizes and gauges. Four-foot-long sections are a common item, and they are usually stocked near the truss plates and joist hangers. These inexpensive pieces have a number of round or oval holes on both faces of the angle iron, giving almost infinite flexibility for installing lag screws pretty much anywhere you like. You can cut the angle iron quickly with a hacksaw into useful lengths: eight inches, twelve inches, or whatever.

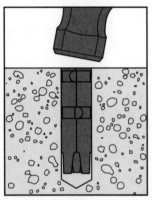

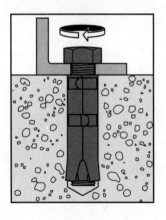

Fig. 4.6: Leaded expansion-shield installation method. Drawing courtesy of Simpson Strong-Tie Co., Inc.

It goes like this: Set the doorframe (or post or sill beam) on the slab, floor, footing or sill. Using a pencil, mark the doorframe's location on whatever surface you are going to fasten to. Choose a length of angle iron a little shorter than the width of the piece you wish to fasten, set it against the pencil line, and choose a couple of appropriate hole locations. Scribe these with a pencil, using the little piece of angle iron as a template. If the receiving surface is concrete, drill appropriately sized holes for whatever anchor you have chosen (leaded expansion shields with lag screw method or strike bolt method). Fasten the angle iron as shown in Figs. 4.6 or 4.7. If you are fastening to a wooden deck, as in Fig. 5.40 on page 136, just drill the appropriate hole into the wood for the lag screw selected.

Now, set the wooden member up next to the angle iron and, with a pencil, scribe a couple of appropriate hole locations on the post, doorframe, or heavy sill. Drill holes into the wooden member, using the correct diameter and depth for the lag screws chosen. Quarter-inch or five-sixteenths-inch screws of two to three inches in length are appropriate. I make my holes in the wood about a quarter-inch less than the full length of the screw below the hex head, and I use a drill of about the same size as the solid shaft (not including threads) of the lag screw. When in doubt, use a smaller size. If this is too tight, you can always make the hole a little bigger. If the screw is too loose and doesn't hold, you will have to drill again nearby, using a smaller hole.

With any lag screwing that you do, it is always wise to test the drill hole size and the screw itself on a piece of similar-species scrap wood. You want a fit that is snug and tight, but not so tight that the wood splits or that it is impossible to turn the screw.

Finally, set the wooden member up again and install the lag screws through the angle iron into the receiving hole in the wood. Snug the screws up with a hex-head ratchet wrench. I particularly like this method when I am unable to lift a post or doorframe over an anchor pin, such as when placing a new member within an existing post-and-beam panel.

Some More About Doorframes and Posts

With a lot of natural building being done these days, cordwood, cob, or straw bale walls of 16 to 24 inches thick are not uncommon. Doorframes will have to be equally wide. Earthwood's cordwood walls are all 16 inches (40.6 centimeters) thick, so I make my doorframes from two four-by-eight timbers, with their 4-inch

(101 millimeter) dimensions butted together, forming, effectively, a 4-by-16-inch door post. These vertical timbers can be fastened together with metal straps, as shown in Fig. 4.54.

Fastening such a doorframe to a concrete floor requires two pins, one for each of the four-by-eights, to stop the doorframe from rotating. Alternatively, a 12- to 16-inch-long piece of angle iron can fasten the frame to the floor as discussed above, and the angle iron is hidden from view in the cordwood wall.

With single posts, such as eight-by-eights, two pins instead of one will stop the post from rotating, and I have mentioned this to students for years. In point of fact, we only used one pin for each of the posts at both Log End Cave and Earthwood, and I have seen no sign of any post rotating. The heavy concentrated load on these posts imparts tremendous friction at each post end, and rotation would be highly unlikely, especially after girders and floors above the posts tie everything together. One pin is enough with heavy structures.

Chris Ryan, like any good builder, likes to use patterns to make jobs easier. My son Rohan helped him set up a corner post at his garage while I took the following sequence of photos:

Fig. 4.8: Chris made a pattern from an eight inch piece of two-by-eight, held it firmly on the corner of his garage footing, and drilled two holes straight down into the plate, already fastened to a course of blocks as described above.

Fig. 4.9: Next, Chris installed a couple of positioning pins into the two-by-eight pressure-treated plate. The pins are made from scrap half-inch (1.2 centimeter) #4 reinforcing bar, or "rebar."

Fig. 4.10: Chris used the pattern to transpose the pin locations to the underside of his eight-by-eight corner posts. In this photo, Chris completes the holes, deep enough so that the post will sit firmly on the sill plate. Rohan and Chris will put the heavy eight-by-eight post in place over the pins seen in Fig. 4.9.

Fig. 4.11: Here, Rohan adjusts the post while Chris checks the plumb bubble of his four-foot level. When the post is plumb, he screws the short brace diagonal into place. The post is plumbed and braced in both directions. One down, about 15 more to go (including four-by-eight doorframe posts.)

In areas of high winds, positioning pins alone may not satisfy local code, and you will probably have to use a code-approved metal fastener for the purpose. But, before we look at these, we should discuss metal fasteners and connectors in a general way.

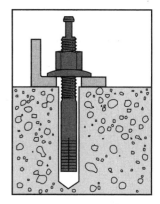
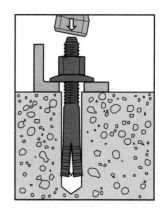

Fig. 4.7: Expansion anchor — or strike bolt — installation method. Drawing courtesy of Simpson Strong-Tie Co., Inc.

Fig. 4.8, top right: Chris made a pattern from an eight inch section of two-by-eight, held it firmly on the corner of his garage footing, and drilled two holes straight down into the plate, already fastened to a course of blocks as described above.

Fig. 4.9, top far right: Next, Chris installed a couple of positioning pins into the two-by-eight pressure-treated plate. The pins are made from scrap half-inch (1.2 centimeter) #4 reinforcing bar, or "rebar."

Fig. 4.10, bottom right: Chris used the pattern to transpose the pin locations to the underside of his eight-by-eight corner posts. In this photo, Chris completes the holes, deep enough so that the post will sit firmly on the sill plate. Rohan and Chris will put the heavy eight-by-eight post in place over the pins seen in Fig. 4.9.

Fig. 4.11, bottom far right: Here, Rohan adjusts the post while Chris checks the plumb bubble of his four-foot level. When the post is plumb, he screws the short brace diagonal into place. The post is plumbed and braced in both directions. One down, about 15 more to go (including four-by-eight doorframe posts.)

About Metal Fasteners

Several companies manufacture metal fasteners for a variety of wood-to-wood and wood-to-foundation applications. Since 1975, I have done a lot of timber framing without using these fasteners (except for truss plates), and I will share my techniques in these pages. But manufactured metal fasteners can make life easier, the building inspector happier, and improve the strength of the structure, so they are a valuable option. There are hundreds of different connectors available, and, while reading this book is a good introduction, I cannot cover all of the products in this relatively small volume. Therefore, you should also 1) go to your local hardware or building supply store and look at what's readily available in your area (see Fig. 4.12) and 2) contact the companies by mail or through the Internet and look at their catalogs or web pages. There is an engineered code-compatible connector for practically every imaginable situation.

If there is a downside to these manufactured connectors and fasteners, it is that they are made mostly for lumber of finished dimensions. In the mechanical fastener industry, a four-by-four is almost always 3½ inches by 3½ inches and a six-by-six is 5½ inches by 5½ inches. However, companies do manufacture full-sized connectors for rough-cut posts, and also some joist hangers for rough-cut material. Simpson Strong-Tie Co, Inc., for example, has joist hangers for all depths (up to 14 inches or 35.6 centimeters) for rough-cut two-bys, four-bys, and six-bys, but not for three-bys and five-bys. One local building supply sells USP joist hangers that will work with full-sized five-by-tens.

Fig. 4.12: There is a great little hardware store in Pahoa, Hawaii, with quite a selection of metal connectors. Practically all new construction in Hawaii makes use of these connectors, because of severe expected wind loads.

Still, over 90 percent of the fasteners in a catalog are for dressed lumber, so you will have to wade carefully through the catalogs to find what you need. You can also call the companies with specific requests, although specialty items will be expensive. Plan ahead for your connectors, so that you have them when you need them. The cost of standard connectors and fasteners is very reasonable, with many simple strap and plate connectors selling for fifty cents or less.

Another potential downside of galvanized metal fasteners is that they are not particularly attractive. However, they are usually installed where they are not seen, or, at any rate, not seen for very long. Also, Simpson Strong-Tie makes a few heavy (12-gauge) ornamental connectors with textured flat black paint, including straps, T-straps, right angles, and a variety of heavy joist hangers. These are quite a bit more expensive than the standard fare, but can justify their cost if only a few are needed in exposed locations.

Post supports, for example, can be installed so that the metal parts will be hidden in the thickness of whatever infilling material is chosen. Similarly, right angle connectors, used, for example, where a girt is supported on a post, can be hidden in the infilling.

Fig. 4.13: George Stuart in Barnardsville, North Carolina, used a homemade T-strap on each side of this post-and-girder join. The girders also have a simple half-lap scarf joint connecting them behind the T-strap, as in Fig. 4.14.

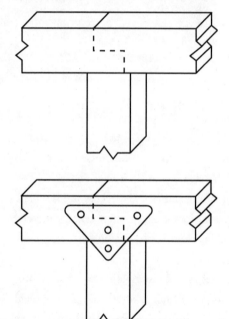

Fig. 4.14a: A simple horizontal half-lap scarf joint. Here, two ten-by-tens join over a ten-by-ten post. Stewart Elliott (1977) says that the post must be two inches (51 millimeters) wider than the length of the lap. This is an easy joint to make, even by inexperienced owner-builders.

Fig. 4.14b: This triangular metal plate with lag screws is a creative alternative to the T-straps of Fig. 4.13. To work properly, there must be an identical plate on each side of the joint.

First floor joists are almost always hidden, but exposed ceiling joists or roof rafters are not.

An option to commercially available fasteners is homemade ones, a favorite of many owner-builders. Several examples are shown in this book. Often, home-made connectors for heavy-timbers are made of one-eighth-inch (3.2 millimeter), three-sixteenth-inch (4.8 millimeter), or one-quarter-inch (6.4 millimeter) flat steel stock, which are all available in regular widths, such as 2-inch, 3-inch, 4-inch, 6-inch, etc. When these steel pieces are painted black, they become an attractive part of the structure. See Figs. 4.13 and 4.14a & b. See also Fig. 5.45 on page 138.

The half-lap joint can cut the girder's shear strength in half, but the frame in Fig. 4.13 is overbuilt in the first place, and the heavy metal plates would return much of the shear strength to the member in any case.

Larry Schuth of Hilton, New York built a cordwood home within a post-and-beam frame, and told of his adventure in Chapter 17 of my previous book, *Cordwood Building: The State of the Art* (see Bibliography), which also has a color picture of the finished home. Larry's foundation consists of two eight-inch block walls laid side by side, in order to provide 16 inches (40.6 centimeters) of bearing for his cordwood. But rather than go "double-wide" with his post system, as Joe Zinni did in Tenino, Washington (see the photo essay Joe's Rocket Research Landing Pad at the end of this chapter), Larry built a strong frame using just single eight-by-eights as seen in Fig. 4.15.

Incidentally, sometimes plywood makes an effective fastener, particularly as gussets (plates that cover an area where two or more timbers come together), and where they can be used in a hidden application.

Wind Can be a Serious Problem...

In certain areas of the country like the southern U.S. Gulf Coast, Hawaii, "Tornado Alley," coastal Alaska, and other areas, code demands a more positive tie-down mechanism than the positioning pin and gravity technique that I employ in northern New York. Fortunately, several manufacturers make a variety of anchoring fasteners whose purpose is to tie the base of the posts to foundations. Three companies are listed in Appendix C. One of the leaders in the field is Simpson Strong-Tie Co., Inc. In their *High-Wind-Resistant Construction Product Selection Guide* (catalog C-HW02, November 1, 2002), on page 4, they say: "Newer building codes such as the International Building Code (IBC), the International Residential Code (IRC), and the Florida Building Code (FBC),

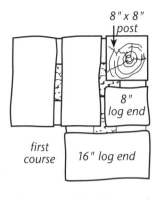

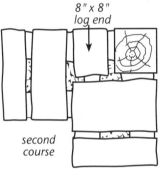

Fig. 4.15: The use of a few short log-ends enabled the Schuths to use a single eight-by-eight-inch post in the corners.

Wind Basics

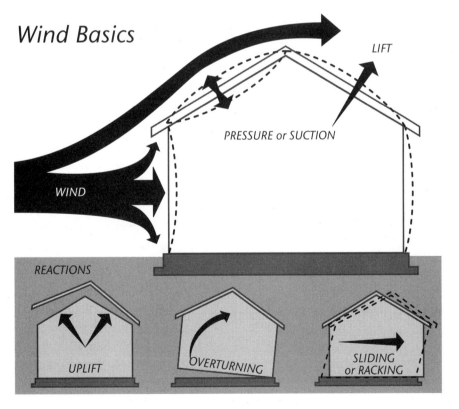

Fig. 4.16: Here, graphically, are the basic ways that wind can affect a structure. Illustration courtesy of Simpson Strong-Tie Co., Inc.

have had a profound effect on the way wind design is performed." The same publication gives this concise overview of how strong winds affect buildings:

During a thunderstorm, blizzard, hurricane, or tornado, the force of the wind on a house works in three ways:

1. As it flows over the roof the wind creates a strong lifting effect (uplift).
2. It exerts horizontal pressure which tries to overturn the structure.
3. If overturning is resisted, the wind pressure tries to slide the structure off of the foundation or to rack the walls.

Be extremely careful working around or under heavy timbers that have not yet been firmly tied to each other and diagonally braced to the ground, foundation, or floor. Avoid timber framing on windy days.

Tying Posts and Sills to the Foundation

Fig. 4.17: Four different post bases. Illustration courtesy of Simpson Strong-Tie Co., Inc.

While codes in areas of severe wind potential are concerned with all the structural components, up to and including tying roof trusses and rafters down to the top plate, the first building requirement will be to tie the posts to the foundation. Simpson makes a variety of post and column bases for the purpose, and some examples are shown in Fig. 4.17, reprinted by kind permission from Simpson. Other companies make similar products. Note that some of these post bases can be fastened to anchor bolts set in the concrete (or in grouted concrete block cores), while others involve embedding the lower part of the base into the concrete. With a poured slab or footing, these anchors will have to be installed accurately at the time of the pour. Make sure that you understand how the base works before you set it up in the concrete, and be careful that the part upon which the post rests is flush with the top of the

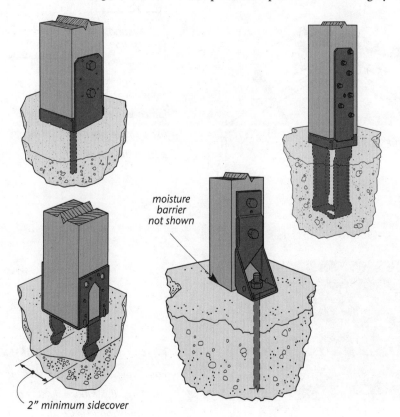

moisture barrier not shown

2" minimum sidecover

foundation or a tiny bit above it. An advantage of the fastener styles that make use of anchor bolts or pins is that the base-support piece is snugged up to the foundation by tightening a hex-headed nut. This system seems a little more forgiving of error.

While visiting Hawaii's Big Island in 2003, I noticed that a lot of people make use of tie-down connectors from the foundation right through to the roof. The Simpson Strong-Tie folks call this a "continuous load transfer path." Steve Sugar says that his building inspector is quite insistent on that, because Hawaii can bare the brunt of some pretty powerful winds. Steve and Eileen Sugar's house, seen in Fig. 4.18, is built up on twenty or so four-by-four posts, each married to heavy concrete bases as shown in Fig. 4.1 at the beginning of the chapter. The metal fasteners were cast in place. The living area is all above the garage space, a protection in case of flooding (in a region of 200-plus inches (5.08 meters) of rain per year) or tsunami (tidal waves) that occasionally hit the coast.

Fig. 4.18: Steve and Eileen Sugar's home in Hawaii makes use of a post-and-beam frame and mechanical fasteners.

On the other side of Hawaii, Terry, another owner-builder, also put his living space eight feet up, and for similar reasons. A self-reliant mango farmer, Terry used strong homemade metal fasteners to tie his main girders to the seven-foot pillars made from concrete-filled hollow-core chimney

Fig. 4.19: The girder is strapped to a concrete-filled column.

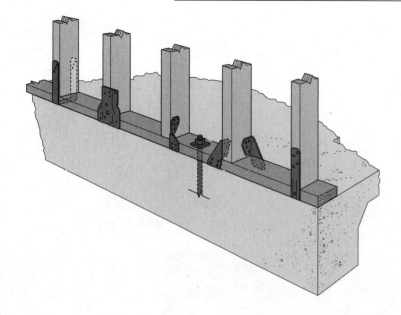

blocks. These blocks, which come in 16- by 16-inch (and other) sizes, are very handy for building a deck up off of the ground. Filling the blocks with concrete and vertical rebar makes a strong pillar, and the U-shaped plate assembly can be set into the concrete of the last core. We see just the exposed part of this assembly in Fig. 4.19. Note, also, that the girder is tied to the main corner post column with a strong metal strap.

We'll return to Hawaii later to see how floor girders and roof rafters were fastened down to posts.

Fig. 4.20: There are a variety of tie-down fasteners and anchors available for joining studs to sills, and sills to foundations. Illustration courtesy of Simpson Strong-Tie Co., Inc.

Specialty fasteners are also available for tying sill plates down to foundations, although regular anchor bolts, as already described, are very strong. In high-wind areas, your tie-down methods will have to agree with local code or the local code-enforcement officer, who may have some discretion. Although *Timber Framing for the Rest of Us* is concerned with post-and-beam framing, not conventional balloon framing, Fig. 4.20 may be of interest to show that fasteners are available for virtually every kind of wood-to-wood (or wood-to-masonry) situation.

Fastening the Girt to the Top of the Posts

Before attempting to lift a heavy girt (or girding beam) to the top of posts, make sure that the posts are vertically plumb — check two adjacent sides with the plumbing bubble on your level — and that all the posts are supported with sturdy bracing, as already discussed. Make sure that the posts are all the same — and the correct — height (see Post Height earlier in this chapter), and that their tops are square, which, in this case, translates to flat.

Based on your plan, the girts might be supported by two, three, or even more posts. A post at each end supports the 16-foot-long (4.9-meter-long) eight-by-eight girts in our garage, with a third post supporting the middle. The posts need to be the same height so that the girt will rest nicely on all three.

Russell Pray, a contractor friend, actually erected our entire garage framework for us while we were conducting workshops in British Columbia. He used a beam-cutting saw (very expensive!) to get nice square cuts on the eight-by-eight and four-by-eight posts and the eight-by-eight girts. To fasten the girts to the top of the posts, he used a heavy-duty electric drill to install ten-inch TimberLok™* screws down through the eight-inch girt and into the tops of the posts, two screws at each post. Lots of temporary diagonal bracing protected the entire frame against racking and provided stability while the 30-foot-long (9.1-meter-long) trusses were installed over the girts. Where two girts butt together over the post halfway along the sidewalls, shorter toe screws at the tops of the girts help tie one to the other.

---

* TimberLok™ screws are made by Olympic Manufacturing Group, Inc. listed in Appendix C. They come in a variety of lengths, with the six-, eight-, and ten-inch (15.2-, 20.3-, and 25.4-centimeter) ones the most useful for timber framing applications. Among the advantages over heavier shank screws and large nails, such as log cabin spikes, is that the TimberLok™ screws install faster and require no pre-drilling; they countersink into the beam; they have a corrosive resistant coating that also helps them grip; and they are easily removable. All TimberLok™ screws have a shank diameter of three-sixteenth inch, and a thread diameter of one-quarter inch. For the long screws, it is recommended to use a high-torque, low (450) rpm drill. Olympic supplies a five-sixteenths inch (8 millimeter) hex head bit with each box of screws. My local supplier sells a box of 50 ten-inch TimberLok™ screws for $28.

GRK Canada, Ltd (also listed in Appendix C), makes an even higher-quality — albeit more expensive — screw of a similar kind.

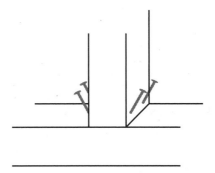

Fig. 4.21: Install toe-nails (or screws) at about a 60-degree angle. As it is driven in, the toenail on the right will drive the post to the left. See sidebar text entitled Toe-nailing and Toe-screwing on the following page.

Toe-nailing and Toe-screwing

Nails, when they became cheap, replaced dowels, dovetails, and mortise-and-tenon joints. Most nailing is called surface nailing: driving a nail straight through one board in order to fasten it to another. This is the way roofing planks and plywood are installed, as well as wooden siding.

But one of the most valuable skills in timber framing for the rest of us is to learn how to toenail properly. A toenail (in carpentry) is a nail driven at an angle that allows us to join one timber to another where they meet at right angles. It is a fairly strong method of nailing, because toenails are always installed opposite each other, as in Fig. 4.21. Some of the nails will always provide shear strength, no matter which way a timber is forced. Toenails don't pull out easily, as you will discover when you make a mistake, and have to take your own work apart.

Toenails should be installed at about a 60-degree angle, as shown in the illustration. With two-by framing, an 8-penny (2.5-inch) toenail is started about three-quarters-inch (1.9 centimeters) up the upright. But with heavy timbers, I tend to use a larger nail, such as a 16-penny (3.5-inch) nail, and start it an inch or even 1.25-inch (3.2 centimeters) up the side of the post. With the 60-degree angle, you will still get plenty of purchase into the wood below.

The "law of the toenail" says that you will move the base of the post or beam in the direction in which you are striking. You can avoid this by marking the post in its correct position with a pencil and then starting one of the toenails until it grabs the substrate. You can drive it until the post begins to move, then stop. Install the opposite toenail as a reactionary thrust. It will move the post back into the correct position. By working on one toenail, then its opposite, you can set the post firmly, right where it belongs.

You can lessen the chance of splitting wood while toe-nailing if, first, you hit the pointy end of a nail quite stiffly with a hammer while its head bears against something hard, such as concrete. This will dull the point. A pointed nail tends to spread the fibers and split the wood, but a blunt nail will simply puncture the wood grain as it penetrates: no split. With large nails, pre-drilling the angle will also reduce the chance of splitting wood and make the nail easier to install.

As the years go by, I use nails less and screws more. Screws have the advantage of being removable. Toe-screwing is my term for using a screw instead of a nail in a toe-nailing situation. With large (3.5- to 4-inch or 10.1 centimeter) deck screws, drill a small pilot hole first to lessen the chance of splitting. Use an electric drill to install these screws, not a screwdriver. Robertson screws — the ones with the little indented squares in the head — drive more positively than Phillips or slotted screws and the heads are less likely to get mangled by the driving bit.

For the remainder of this book, the terms "toenail" or "toenailing" also implies the optional use of screws.

Toenailing can also be used to fasten any beam over a post. The toenails (or screws) are driven upward through the post into the beam. See the sidebar on the facing page. The "law of the toenail" is particularly strong in this situation, and screws give a little more control than nails.

Another way to hold the beam fast over a post as by the use of truss plates, as shown in Fig. 4.22a, and you really need to place one each side of the wall to get the proper strength. The downside of this method is that the truss plates will often be in view in this application, and they are not particularly nice looking. You can beat this by making your own heavy (one-eighth-inch or 3.2 millimeter) pieces, drilling holes in them, and installing them as in Fig. 4.22b, with, say, two one-quarter-inch by 3-inch (0.6- by 7.6-centimeter) lag screws into each member (four per plate, each side of the joint.) Paint them whatever color tickles you. But black is nice.

Yet another post-to-beam fastening method is shown in Fig. 4.22c, in which the metal can be hidden inside of an infilled wall. Here, right-angle fasteners, commonly available at any hardware store, are used instead of toenails. These are like ordinary truss plates, but bent in the middle to form a right-angle. In a pinch, I have bent truss plates into right angles for the purpose, as in Fig. 4.35. Use four-penny (4d) nails, which are one-and-a-half inches long. You don't have to put a nail in every hole provided. I generally use about half the holes, as long as this is at least five in number, more with larger plates or right-angle fasteners.

When Two Beams Meet Over a Post...

Where any two beams meet over a post, there are many ways, short of matrimony, to join them together. Traditional timber framers have a variety of joints to use in this situation, including an assortment of "scarf" and "dovetail" joints — these take practice — and half-lap joints, as in Fig. 4.14. Lap joints are not too difficult to make with common tools, and you may like to have a go at them. A drawback, however, is that shear strength of the beam is diminished when it is cut half way through. In fact, weakening of structural members is almost always the case with any traditional joint. Another example of this would be an eight-by-eight-inch beam with a tenon of two-by-eight-inch cross-section carved into its end for insertion into the mortise of an adjacent post. Shear strength is reduced by 75 percent in this case. This is not a problem for timber framers because the structures are so extraordinarily over-built in the first place, and good tight-fitting joints and pegs go a long ways towards promoting strong joints.

The rest of us have several choices:

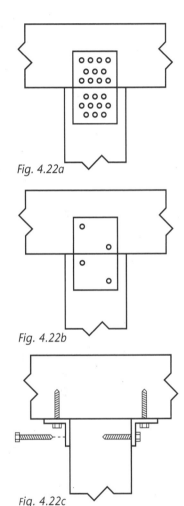

Fig. 4.22a

Fig. 4.22b

Fig. 4.22c

Fig. 4.22: Three different methods of fastening a beam over a post. (Fig. 4.22c shows a method using an angle iron and lag screws similar to Fig. 5.40.)

Fig. 4.23, above: Truss plates tie the girders together at the octagonal internal frame at Earthwood. This frame cuts the radial floor joist spans in half.

Fig. 4.24, right: Two four-by-ten (10.1- by 25.4-centimeter) girders meet over a four-by-four post, the joint made strong by the use of a pair of galvanized metal connectors.

1. Truss plates on the top. I used this method to join the tops of the post-supported octagonal ring beam at Earthwood. This octagon, halfway between the center pillar and the external walls, cuts the floor joist spans in half on the first floor, and the roof rafter span in half on the second story. When you cut its span in half, you make a beam — remember? — four times stronger on bending. The truss plates are out of the way and out of view, so this was an effective solution. See Fig. 4.23.

2. Toe-nailing or toe-screwing from the top of one horizontal timber, diagonally into the end of the adjacent member. Not quite as rigid as the truss plate method, but quite strong just the same, and useful where truss plates will either be seen or be in the way of fastening another post or beam.

3. T-straps. (Figs. 4.13, 4.24 and 4.25) You can buy a variety of these at the building supply, and their esthetic qualities vary. My friend Steve in Hawaii used the off-the-shelf connectors shown in Fig. 4.24 to join two four-by-ten girders over a four-by-four post. This pair of connectors does everything in one shot: it connects the two girders, and connects the girders to the post. It is not beautiful, but the detail is down in the garage, under the living space, so esthetics matter less. Esthetically, the best T-straps I have seen are homemade as shown in Fig. 4.13 and use lag screws instead of nails. Several acquaintances have made their own attractive T-straps from one-eighth-inch stock or better, and painted them black. Whenever this method is used, full strength comes from using them on both sides of the joint. Some manufacturers make decorative heavy strap connectors, too.

4. A simple notch. Sometimes, as we have seen, a little simple notching can be quite useful. Larry Schuth wanted his posts to carry right on through two stories on the high side of his saltbox design, in order to make his frame more rigid. Fig. 4.26 shows where the post goes through the floor of the loft. Using a circular saw and a chisel, Larry has carefully removed a 1½- by 8-inch (3.8- by 20.3-centimeter) notch of wood from each side of his post, so that girders — also eight-by-eights — can be let into the post. Heavy angle iron braces complete the join, as seen in Figs. 4.26 and 4.22c.

5. Capital. A "capital" is a block used to distribute the load from more than one beam onto a post, usually because the post is lacking in space to accommodate the bearing of two or more timbers. Geoff Huggins joined two built-up eight-by-twelve oak girders over his post by transferring the load through a heavy block of wood, the capital. (Fig. 4.27) At our 20-foot (6-meter)-diameter office building, I used a 24-inch (61-centimeter) octagonal capital over a 9-inch (22.8-centimeter)-diameter post, so that all of the 16 five-by-ten radial rafters had room to join in the center. See Fig. 4.28.

Fig. 4.25, top: Larry Schuth joined two girts over a post, using homemade connectors made from 3- by 3-inch (7.6- by 7.6-centimeter) by one-quarter-inch (6.4 millimeter) angle iron and some one-quarter-inch plate steel, all from a salvage yard. You can also see four-by-six-inch roof rafters supported by the girt and a six-by-six-inch tie beam, which ties the two long walls of his saltbox home together, preventing outward spread by the rafters. Larry Schuth photo.

Fig. 4.26, center: Two girders are notched into this eight-by-eight post, and support six-by-six floor joists and a six-by-six tie beam. Angle-iron supports hold the joint together. A joist, the post, and a tie beam are all fastened together by a single piece of one-half-inch threaded rod, with washers and nuts at each end. You can see the end of this rod and a nut at the upper right. Larry Schuth photo.

Fig. 4.27, bottom: Geoff Huggins used a capital on top of his post, to provide plenty of bearing surface where two eight-by-twelve built-up girders come together.

Maintain a whole toolbox of these joining methods and have them all available for use as needed. Sometimes one method won't work but another will. Redundancy of methods is not necessarily a bad thing, either. With large projects, in fact, good engineers deliberately incorporate structural redundancy into buildings to allow loads to be carried by more than one path.

Fig. 4.28: At the Earthwood office, 16 five-by-ten radial rafters join over an octagonal capital. The capital, 12 inches (30.5 centimeters) high by 24 inches (61.0 centimeters) in diameter, is made from four pieces of six-by-twelve timber, with consecutive courses criss-crossed at 90 degrees to each other. The pieces are fastened together with 10-inch (25.4-centimeter) log cabin spikes, eight in all. An extra benefit of a capital like this one, or the one in Fig. 4.27, is that the true, clear span of the beams is effectively reduced by a few inches, increasing both shear and bending strength.

Timber Framing Hybrid

Let's return to Chris Ryan's garage to see a method of making girts from a pair of two-by-eights instead of a single eight-by-eight. Chris had seen that Russell Pray used a similar method on the gables ends of the garage at Earthwood and he modified Russell's method slightly, so that he could use doubled two-by-eights all around the building at the girt level. The advantages were twofold: 1) he was able to save on cost, as two two-by-eights are only half as much wood as a single eight-by-eight. And, 2) Chris could install the two-by-eights working alone, whereas hefting long heavy eight-by-eight girts up over the eight-foot-high posts would require a crew of helpers.

This hybrid method of timber framing is very strong. It is not quite traditional timber framing, as it does use some metal fasteners and the joints are easy to make with a circular saw and a chisel. But it requires shaping the top of posts. "Timber framing for the rest of us" does not mean that you have to be afraid of a little timber shaping. I always get a lot of satisfaction when I take the time to make a simple wood joint, even the relatively easy kind described here. Figs. 4.29 through 4.36 will take you through the simple process.

Fig. 4.29: The goal is to support a doubled system of continuous full-sized two-by-eights all around the building at the girt level. One set will be installed flush with the posts on the inside, and the other set will be flush with the posts on the outside. To accomplish this, all that is needed is to remove some of the wood at the top of the post to create a notch — or "shoulder" — upon which the two-by-eight will be supported. Here, Chris works on the top of a four-by-eight door frame. He marks a notch eight inches (20.3 centimeters) long and two inches (5.1 centimeters) from each edge of the eight-inch (20.3-centimeter)-wide surface of the post. He cuts as deeply as he can with his circular saw, then turns the timber over and repeats from the other side. Then he makes the transverse cut across the four-inch dimension. This one can be done at the full two-inch depth.

Fig. 4.30: The two longer cuts meet, but not quite all the way, because of the circular shape of the saw blade. However, the wood is easily snapped off with a chisel.

Fig. 4.31: The four eight-by-eight corner posts have two inches of wood removed all the way around the top of the post, down to a shoulder eight inches from the top. Again, this is accomplished by combining saw cuts with chisel work. All of the post tops for the garage are shaped in this way before they are stood up and plumbed, but sidewall posts need shoulders on just the inner and outer sides, not all four.

Fig. 4.32: Here, the three major eight-by-eight posts along the sidewall are in place. The middle post is set to the stretched nylon mason's line. Corner posts are shaped as in the previous picture, Fig. 4.31, and the middle eight-by-eight has had just its sides trimmed back two inches to receive the two-by-eights, butted together on the shoulder.

Fig. 4.33: Two outside two-by-eights, each 14 feet long, meet over the middle post, which is another eight-by-eight. It is the fourth one from the left. The other two posts, with a door lintel notched in near the top, are made of four-by-eights, as shown in Figs. 4.34 and 4.35. This view shows clearly where the inner two-by-eight member of this girt system will bear on the notched posts.

Fig. 4.34: This detail shows the notching of the door lintel into the doorposts. The four-inch-thick lintel is set about 1-1/2 inches (3.8 centimeters) into the four-inch dimension of the posts. Four-inch (10.1-centimeter) screws driven from the side of the post into the lintel could hold it in place, as could four-inch (20-penny) nails. Screws have less impact on the frame than nails, and they are easily removed.

Fig. 4.35, far right: This is the other side of Fig. 4.34. Chris used right-angle galvanized metal connectors to hold the lintel fast to the door posts.

Fig. 4.36: The two-by-eights at the gable ends give stability to the entire rectilinear frame of the garage. One of the two-by-eights needs to be attached with a mechanical fastener or toenails. The little piece replaces a chiseled cut from Fig. 4.31 that really did not have to be removed in the first place. If this was an error, it was a very minor one, and gave Chris the option of fastening the doubled two-by-eights in two different ways. Visualization is important in planning even simple joints. Draw everything out on paper first, erasing and redrawing lines until it makes sense.

Build Quality, Gravity and Inertia

Note that in all of the joining methods described above, the beams are not diminished in cross-section, so full shear and bending strength is maintained.

I cannot over-emphasize the importance of maintaining a good standard of "build quality." One member should bear flat on another, without wobbling. The end of a beam should bear at least four inches on the supporting post or beam below, if possible. Timbers should be vertically plumb and horizontally level. The design should assure that the line of thrust is always transferred directly in compression from one member to another.

By paying attention to the build quality, you enlist a great ally, which is the force of gravity. Gravity is very precise: it always works exactly vertically (which enables a bubble-level to function properly, by the way). And it is reliable; that is to say, it is working for you every morning when you wake up, and through the night as well.

Gravity and its close relative inertia are very important parts of all heavy timber-framed structures. Earth-roofed structures help even more in this regard. Our roof at Earthwood weighs between 60 and 120 tons, depending on moisture and snow loads. Even at the low end (dry, no snow), the 60-ton load has a tremendous inertia. The seven load-bearing eight-by-eight posts downstairs are not even pinned to the floor; with at least three tons on each post, they aren't going anywhere. (I know, three times seven tons is only 21 tons. The external walls and central masonry column support the rest.) Now, I don't advise not pinning the posts to the floor — "Do as I say, not as I do!" — but I just thought you might find our experience interesting.

Gravity can work against you, too. You have probably seen lots of diagrams like Fig. 4.37. These drawings depict freestanding cordwood walls, which are strong on compression and weak on tension. Using cordwood exaggerates the effect of the stresses a bit, but helps make the point. The same sorts of compression and tension forces are at play in a post-and-beam wall. They may be less obvious, but they need to be attended to for the same reasons.

In Fig. 4.37a, the roof load wants to follow gravity's path, but the angle of the rigid rafters transfers the downward thrust to an outward thrust on the walls, and the building falls down. This would be an excellent example of egregiously bad build quality. In Fig. 4.37b, the tie beam has a tensile strength sufficient to offset

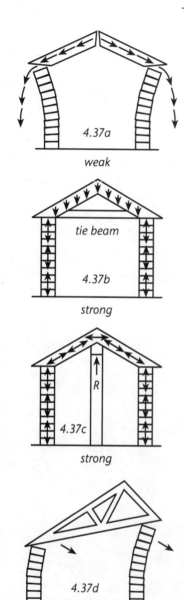

4.37a

weak

tie beam

4.37b

strong

R

4.37c

strong

4.37d

weak

the outward thrust. Another way of thinking about it is that the tie beam turns the roof structure into a giant rigid triangle, a triangle with — and this is important — a flat bottom. Gravity's downward thrust is carried straight down onto the vertical walls. This is how trusses work.

In Fig. 4.37c, rafters are well-tied to a ridge beam, which, in turn, is supported by posts. If the tops of the rafters can't go down — and they can't because of the reactionary load "R" provided by the posts — then they cannot put an outward thrust on the walls.

The importance of level and plumb is illustrated in Fig. 4.37d. Here, we have a nice rigid triangular truss, but the bottom chord of the truss, which is inclined, alters the vertical line of thrust. This resultant vector of force places unacceptable stresses on the walls, as shown. Working with gravity, and not against it, is always a good idea. In this example, if the walls were the same height, and the bottom chord was horizontal, the line of thrust would be straight down onto the walls, which — being strong on compression — would then provide the required reactionary load.

Build quality, gravity, and inertia can be important allies … or deadly enemies.

Roof Systems

There are basically two different roof-support systems that are appropriate for use with timber framing. Most timber framers continue on with additional timber framing, and I have done this, as well, at Log End Cottage, Log End Cave, and Earthwood, by using methods described in this book. The other support system that should be considered carefully is the truss-supported roof, like the garage at Earthwood and the one that Chris built.

Is one system better than the other? Not necessarily. There are pros and cons for each.

1. **Engineering**. Trusses are normally designed and built by professionals. I'm not saying that owner-builders have never done it, and successfully, but, like mixing one's own concrete, it is hardly worth the effort for the money saved. Engineering is crucial. You would need to use a standard truss design that happens to suit the dimensions and purpose of your building, or have the trusses professionally engineered. Then you'd need to create a large template, such as on a barn floor, to actually fasten the various chords together with truss plates. Purchased trusses are not that

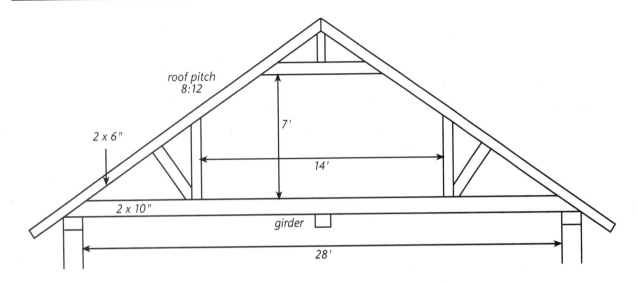

Fig. 4.38: Richard Flatau's attic trusses looked something like this.

expensive, and the manufacturers know how to design a truss for your application.

The engineering of a timber-framed roof is a bit more basic, and timber frame designs tend to be on the over-built side, anyway. With a rafter system, you can consult span tables to find appropriate timber size. Still, unless you are following a tried and proven plan, you should have your entire timber-frame plan checked by a structural engineer. And strong jointing, both at the top and the bottom of the rafter, is critical.

2. **Upstairs space**. With timber framing, it is, perhaps, a little easier to create useful space under the roof, although there is a truss design, called "attic trusses" which can afford some space upstairs, usually a little less than half of the entire area of the ceiling below. Richard Flatau used attic trusses with his post-and-beam cordwood home in Merrill, Wisconsin. The company that engineered, built, and delivered the trusses also put them up onto the girts. Their delivery truck has a boom built onto it for the purpose. Richard hired a contractor friend experienced in truss work and enlisted a couple of other friends as "grunts," and the 20 heavy trusses were installed in just two hours. Richard says that the trusses enclose 560 square feet (52 square meters) of extra living space upstairs, including two bedrooms, a play area, ample storage, and a half bath. See Fig. 4.38.

3. **Ease of construction**. By the time the girts are in place, timber-framing the roof structure will be an extension of using many of the same

techniques with which the builder is already familiar, although there will be a few new ones. Trusses are an entirely different kettle of fish, but installing trusses is not that difficult, particularly if you follow Richard Flatau's example and hire one person with experience to tell you and your other helpers what to do.

Trusses can be installed with or without the use of a crane. Chris Ryan simply had his garage trusses delivered to site, and he and two friends were able to hang them upside down between the parallel sidewalls by themselves. (Fig. 4.46 on page 97). Later, with a man at the top of each side wall, a third person with a long pole would "flip" a truss upright, and then, from a ladder, help the team space and brace the truss into position. It is really important that the trusses be square on the girt system, parallel to each other, and exactly at the planned regular spacing, usually 16 or 24 inches on center.

Using a framing square, you should mark the top of each girt, showing each edge of each truss. Make sure the spacing comes out right on both sides. Spacing is critical if you are planning to nail plywood on top, or sheetrock ceilings to the underside of the trusses. Squareness and plumb are both part of the all-important build quality.

On balance, and assuming that you find someone with experience to help, I'd say that trusses are probably quicker and easier than timber framing.

Incidentally, traditional timber framers often create what can be described as timber-framed trusses, which they raise like bents on the day of the timber raising, as we saw back in Fig. 2.17. Conventional timber framers — the rest of us — usually install each member individually.

4. **Cost.** Richard Flatau says that his attic trusses actually cost $800 less (1979 prices) than the cost of a conventional "stick-built" roof. The total cost of his 20 trusses, delivered and placed on the girts, was $1,400 in 1979. These were large, heavy trusses, suitable to support floor loads upstairs. I think it is safe to just about triple the cost of those trusses today. Our garage trusses span 24 feet and have two-foot overhangs each side, and cost us $58 each in 1998. But Richard's trusses were made from two-by-sixes and two-by-tens, while all parts of our trusses are two-by-fours. It is difficult to compare truss cost to timber-frame cost, as the cost of the timbers themselves varies so widely from one project to another, depending on

how the timbers were procured. While trusses may be cheaper than conventional stick-frame construction (when labor is factored in), they are certainly more expensive than framing with homegrown timbers.

Roof Timber Framing for the Rest of Us

Ridge beam. I cannot hide my love for a substantial ridge beam (also called, correctly but oddly, a ridgepole), and I'm not talking about the comparatively flimsy ridge "board" used by most stick-frame builders. No, I like something like the eight-by-ten at Log End Cottage (Fig. 4.39) or the ten-by-ten at Log End Cave (Fig. 4.40). Both of these houses were designed to support heavy earth roof loads, so the ridge beam spans were limited to about ten feet. Internal posts can be "free-standing," where they are not in the way, or they can be incorporated into a wall and become integral with the floor plan. At Earthwood, we have two free-standing posts, one each story, and we learn to live and work around them. Another is built into a kitchen peninsula, containing countertop and cabinets beneath.

The post-supported ridge beam is strong. It transfers the load down in compression through the posts. As usual, brace the posts so that they are sturdy and plumb. I use screws to fasten the bracing material. Compared with pounding — and removing — nails, screwing imparts less stress to the frame. Sidewall posts can generally be braced to stakes in the ground, but on concrete brace as shown in Fig. 4.41.

Carefully measure and mark the rafter location along the ridge beam and also along the sidewall girts, according to your plan.

Rafters can be hung on the ridge beam with rafter hangers, but, as the hangers are adjustable for different pitches, they tend to be quite uncommon, as well as expensive. Another method is to notch the rafters into the ridge beam. At Log End Cottage, we were fortunate that our recycled eight-by-ten ridge beam was already notched to receive the three-by-ten rafters that we recycled from the

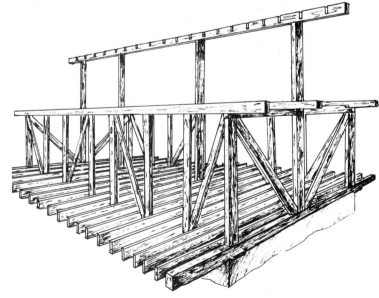

Fig. 4.39: This was the post-and-beam frame for Log End Cottage. The ridge beam was a recycled eight-by-ten and already notched to receive the three-by-ten rafters, not shown. The roof slope is 8:12. Drawing by Marie Cyburt Taluba.

Fig. 4.40: Here, all of the east side four-by-eight rafters at Log End Cave are in place, with their western (right) ends supported over 30-foot-long ten-by-ten central girder or ridge beam. This ridge beam is well-supported along its length by a total of four posts, one at each end, and two others along the way to shorten the spans.

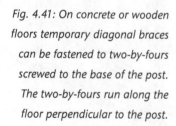

Fig. 4.41: On concrete or wooden floors temporary diagonal braces can be fastened to two-by-fours screwed to the base of the post. The two-by-fours run along the floor perpendicular to the post.

same 19th century building in our local village.

Yet another good method is to join a corresponding pair of rafters over the ridge beam, as we did at Log End Cave. In this case, truss plates on each side of the four-by-eights, at the ridge, can tie each pair of rafters together, or a metal strap can be installed over the top of the rafters, which also serves to tie the rafters to each other. This is important; whatever method of fastening you choose, the rafters must be positively fastened to the ridge beam or to each other to prevent a lateral thrust on the walls. Explanation: The ridge beam cannot move in a downward direction because of the "reactionary load" of the posts, as we saw in Fig. 4.37c. If the rafters are firmly fastened at the ridge, their top ends cannot move downward either. If the tops of the rafters cannot move downwards, the lower parts of the rafters cannot splay the sidewalls outwards.

Fastening rafters to sidewalls using birdsmouths. There are various ways of tying rafters to sidewalls, and the choices may vary depending on roof pitch. One of the most common is the use of "birdsmouths" cut into the rafter. A notch is cut into the rafter so that the rafter bears down flat upon the doubled top plate of stick framing, or upon the girt in heavy timber framing. (The notch resembles a bird's open beak, thus the term.) The birdsmouthing method, in combination with toe-nailing or the use of metal right angle fasteners, is a good way to transfer load down to the wall with roof slopes of 2:12 to 12:12. But there are drawbacks:

1. The rafter is weakened when you cut into its cross section in this way, particularly on shear, which is a function of cross-sectional area of the timber. This weakness is mostly in the overhang.

2. It is very easy to make a mistake and cut the birdsmouth at the wrong location. Either the piece is wasted, or there will be some other problem with the build quality if you try to use a miscut member. One would like to think that each piece should be exactly the same, and that a template that works well for one rafter will work for all. In the best of all possible worlds, this is true, but combine rough-cut material with a first-time owner-builder, and the chances of success with a template are pretty slim. By all means, use a template for marking the depth and shape of the cut according to the chosen pitch, but be ready to change the distance spacing of the birdsmouth from the ridge according to actual (not theoretical) measurements. I used a template at Log End Cave (Fig. 4.42), but always checked my measurements for each rafter, sliding the template a little bit, as needed, to accommodate discrepancies.

3. Rafters with birdsmouths in them are not much use for recycling when another builder attempts to recycle your materials two hundred years from now.

4. The cuts are moderately difficult on heavy timbers, such as five-by-tens, something we're trying to avoid with timber framing for the rest of us.

Fig. 4.42: I mark the birdsmouth on a four-by-eight rafter by using a template made from a one-by-eight board.

You may have guessed that I'm not a big fan of birdsmouths, although I used them on the three-by-ten rafters at Log End Cottage in 1975. I remember that it was a slow tedious process, for reasons already stated in Drawback 2 above. But, in fairness, it must be stated that birdsmouthing is the method that most carpenters use.

Metal connectors are not commonly made for replacing birdsmouthing, and the reason for this may be that connectors would have to be made for a variety of pitches. However, metal tie-down connectors for use in special wind or seismic

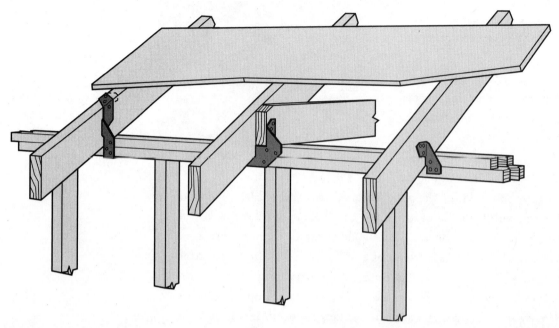

Fig. 4.43: A variety of tie-down connectors. Illustration courtesy of Simpson Strong-Tie Co., Inc.

areas are very common and will be required by code in those areas. They can be used in combination with birdsmouths. Examples of such tie-down connectors are shown in Fig. 4.43.

Fastening rafters to sidewalls using shims. With shallow-sloped roofs, — say 1:12 to 2:12 — I avoid birdsmouths altogether in favor of shimming with wooden shingles. These shingles, usually white cedar, have a taper to them of about one-quarter in twelve (0.25:12). So four shingles, laid one upon another, yields a 1:12-slope roof, which I like with plank-and-beam earth roofs. The use of shingles with rough-cut timbers has these advantages:

1. It is easy to accommodate different depth dimensions of the rafters with shims. Extra shims can raise "low" rafters so that tops of all are in the same plane, greatly facilitating the installation of planking or plywood.
2. Shimming is much easier to do than birdsmouthing, and yet is still strong, because of the great friction between the rough wood shingles and rough-cut timbers.
3. The use of shims does not weaken the rafters in shear, particularly important with heavy earth roof loads.

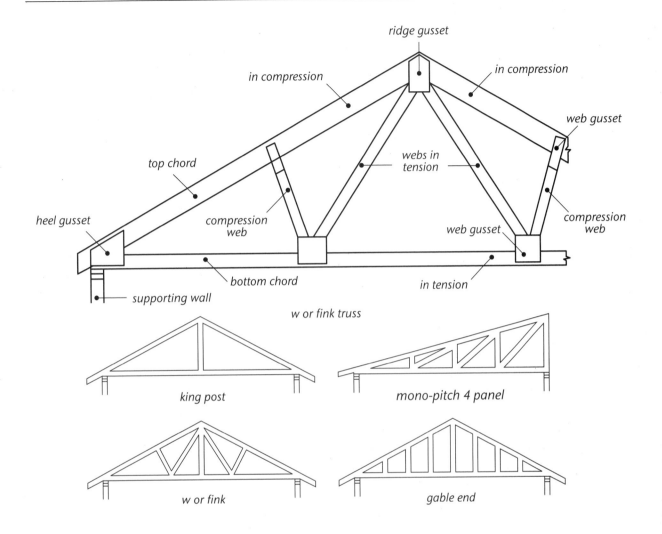

Fig. 4.44: Trusses. Top: Typical W truss, showing its parts and how they work. Bottom: Various truss designs satisfy different needs. Here are just four common ones. Reproduced from Residential Framing by William P. Spence (©1993 by William P. Spence) with permission from Sterling Publishing Co., Inc., NY, NY 10016.

4. A place of common error is eliminated, saving the heartbreak of a wasted timber. (Hey, it's heartbreak for me, known for squeezing a quarter until the eagle screeches.)

After the rafters are all shimmed and placed in the right locations (which you've already marked with pencil on the girt), you can use toenails or right-angle plates to tie them to the wall. Remember that in certain areas, code may require metal straps or metal tie-downs to tie the roof structure to the wall structure, part of the continuous load path already discussed.

More About Trusses

While trusses may be a little off the title subject of this book, they can be an easy, quick, and relatively economic method of building a roof, and they marry well to a strong one- or two-story post-and-beam framework. Trusses can be engineered for a variety of roof shapes, as seen in Fig. 4.44. They are great for garages, and are frequently used now in housing. Normally, there is no attic space in a trussed roof, but, as we have seen, the use of special "attic trusses" can yield quite a bit of upstairs space. Attic trusses will be heavier and more expensive, because the bottom chord of the truss has to be strong enough to support living space. But the extra cost is quite effective on a "square foot per dollar" basis.

Manufactured trusses are not particularly pretty, but, since they are normally hidden, this isn't really a problem. Ceilings can be applied to the underside of the trusses, and you can install blanket or blown-in insulation in the spaces between. So, although you won't see any beautiful beams overhead, you can have a light-colored ceiling to brighten the whole building, and plenty of easy insulation options.

It is important that trusses be stored vertically, or on a flat slab. Storing them on rough ground is the worst situation, as it puts all sorts of unwanted stresses on the truss plates, stresses that they are not meant to endure.

Let's have a last look (with Figures 4.45–4.51) at Chris Ryan's garage project, where three people were able to install the 28-foot-long (8.5-meter-long) trusses without difficulty.

Fig. 4.45: These engineered trusses are strong even for our North Country snow loads, but are made from two-by-fours, so they are not very heavy.

Plank and Beam Roofing

"Plank and beam" roofing consists of planks — often tongue-in-groove — supported from below by exposed beams, or rafters. This is the system we used at Log End Cottage, Log End Cave, and Earthwood, and it is my favorite roof support system for three reasons:

1. We like the aesthetic appeal of exposed beams, with light-colored V-joint tongue-in-groove planking above them.

Fig. 4.46: The trusses are temporarily stored upside down, straddling the sidewalls.

Fig. 4.47: Chris started with the second truss from the end, well braced to the ground. The first and last trusses, called the gable trusses, have overhangs built into them, which makes them more difficult to deal with. After all the other trusses are braced firmly in place, the two gable trusses are installed. The 24-inch centers are already marked on the sidewall girts, and each truss is given exactly the same overhang at each end. Once the overhang has been determined at both ends of the first truss, the others can be marked exactly the same. Before the crew arrived, Chris made sure that his sidewalls were straight and well-braced from the sides.

2. Plank and beam roofing is strong. For example, two-by-six tongue-in-groove planking — on four-foot centers — will support a 185 PSF (pounds per square foot) earth roof load, providing that the beam framework is engineered correctly. With conventional roof loads, planking spans of six feet and even eight feet are possible. Fig. 4.52 shows a strong homemade truss system, with the tension and compression web members sandwiched

Fig. 4.48: With a long two-by-four fastened near the top of the truss with a pivot nail, Chris raises the point of the truss to vertical. The two helpers set it on the 24-inch center marks, and communicate with each other about the overhang. Toenails fasten the trusses to the doubled two-by-eight girts, but the trusses are also temporarily cross-braced to each other, so that they don't go down like so many dominoes.

Fig. 4.49: The third truss is raised.

between doubled top and bottom chords. Note the wide planking spans and the attractive heavy metal truss plates.

Incidentally, building up a frame with bolted timbers, as in this picture, is another great framing system, but beyond the scope of this book. Called the Walter Segal timber frame method, it has become very popular with owner-builders in the United Kingdom. The method is covered very well in *Out of the Woods: Ecological Designs for Timber Frame Housing*, listed in the Bibliography.

Fig. 4.50: Chris and his wife, Kat, make and install the "ladder" to the two gable trusses, to provide an overhang. Note that the gable trusses have lots of vertical members, instead of the angled tension and compression chords. With the ladder and number of vertical members, these trusses are probably about twice as heavy as the others. They can be installed after the other trusses are well-braced to each other.

Fig. 4.51: The last truss, a gable truss, is braced in place. Once the trusses are in place, roofing options are to install horizontal boards called "purlins" and metal roofing, or the entire roof can be planked or decked with plywood for installation of shingles.

3. Plank and beam roofing is easy to do. Nailing goes quickly because normally, the installer is nailing into fairly wide beams. You've almost got to try to miss the beam to do so.

Once the plank-and-beam roof is engineered, installation is as easy as installing the rafters, then nailing down the planking.

Insulating Plank and Beam Roofing

Insulating a plank-and-beam roof is a little different than other styles without exposed beams. Log End Cottage had a fairly steep roof, with a slope of about eight-in-twelve (8:12). In that home, the "beam" component consisted of full-sized recycled three-by-tens. We planked over this with ordinary one-inch planking from the sawmill, planed one side for regularity of thickness, as well as for smoothness and appearance on the exposed interior. To insulate, we created a "double roof." On the topside of the planking, over each of the three-by-tens, we installed a plastic vapor barrier and then another rafter made from a full-sized two-by-six.

We insulated between the two-by-six rafters with fiberglass batt insulation, and then installed a second layer of one-by planking, upon which our roofing material was affixed. This worked pretty well, but I made a couple of mistakes. First, I didn't vent the space properly. Installed correctly, there should be about two inches of air above the fiberglass batts, and this space should be vented from below, at the eaves, by way of soffit venting, and at the ridge by a ridge vent, a fairly standard item used on peaked shingled roofs of this kind. Allowing for the vented air space above the insulation, I would have needed two-by-eights for the topmost rafter system. Second, we should have immediately closed off the soffits (space between rafters at the eaves) with rodent-proof venting, such as quarter-inch grid wire mesh (also called hardware cloth), or wooden soffits with soffit vents made for the purpose — another common item at building supply yards. As it was, we had squirrels living in our roof during the three years we lived at the Cottage. They are fairly irritating, although, from their point of view, I should imagine that they were cozy through the winter.

Shallow-pitched plank and beam roofs can be insulated in the same way as a steeply pitched roof, but I much prefer the use of rigid foam insulation

Fig. 4.52: Strong trusses, built on site, support a plank roof.

with shallow-pitched roofs, and I'll show you how we did this on our new addition, the "case study" subject of the next chapter.

I'll conclude this chapter with an impressive example of an owner-builder employing timber framing techniques "for the rest of us."

Joe's Rocket Research Landing Pad – A Photo Essay

Joe Zinni, like Larry Schuth and Mark Powers, is a former cordwood masonry student at Earthwood. He and his wife Glenna found a 1.25-acre piece building lot they liked in Tenino, Washington, an area where local sawmills are cutting lots of very large timbers. Joe described a friend's sawmill to me: "Rob, picture a giant Wood Mizer mill, except with a band saw blade eight inches wide and a quarter inch thick, and a throat about six feet across. You wouldn't believe the size of the timbers they run through there." In a letter, Joe listed some timbers he has lying around. One is a 16- by 32-inch by 40-foot (40.6- by 81.3-centimeter by 12.2-meter) beam. Another is 13- by 40-inch by 36-feet long. He's got a half dozen beams measuring 12- by 26-inches by 40 feet. The mind boggles. I have megalithic fantasy dreams about the structures I could design around these behemoths.

His own house is 40 feet (12.2 meters) square and framed with large timbers: sixteen-by-sixteen corner posts, eight-by-sixteen sidewall posts (built up from two eight-by-eights strapped to each other, side by side), a double course of six-by-twelves as girts above the posts, and two rows of eight-by-sixteen girders running through the house to shorten ceiling joist spans. The joists themselves are six-by-twelves, and they support two-by-six tongue-in-groove planking. Once the deck was on, the place had become somewhat of a local legend, like a Neolithic "Woodhenge." As "Woodhenge" probably wouldn't mean a lot to locals, Joe put up a sign outside the project which all could understand: Joe's Rocket Research Landing Pad.

Because of high earthquake potential, the building codes in Joe's area insist on a strong foundation-to-roof tie system. Joe used off-the-shelf Simpson strap ties, and, in exposed areas, heavy angle-iron brackets. His fine pictures (Figs. 4.53–4.62) tell the story.

Fig. 4.53: Joe Zinni's floating slab
for his 40- by 40-foot (12.2- by
12.2-meter) cordwood- and-
timber-frame home. Dozens of
heavy timbers are stacked off the
ground on wooden stickers.
Joe Zinni photo.

Fig. 4.54: Joe's sidewall posts are made of
two eight-by-eights, strapped together
with Simpson ties. The entire post is
anchored to the concrete foundation with
a Simpson HPAHD "holdown." A code-
required damp-proof course is installed
between the post and the concrete.
Joe Zinni photo.

Fig. 4.55: Corner posts are full-
sized 16- by 16-inch (40.6- by
40.6-centimeter) timbers. Girts
connecting the tops of the posts
are six-by-twelves. Joe joined the
girts at the corners with 45-degree
miter cuts, a nice detail. Each post
is well-staked to the ground, and
the top girt is eyeballed straight.
Joe Zinni photo.

Fig. 4.56: Joe Zinni fastens one six-by-twelve timber to another with two large lag screws. Joe Zinni photo.

Fig. 4.57: The basic post and beam frame is almost completed. Joe Zinni photo.

Fig. 4.58. Joe's Rocket Research Landing Pad is ready for a rocket to land. The plank roof will receive the roof trusses. Joe Zinni photo.

Fig. 4.59: The roof trusses have a 10-foot (3-meter) cantilevered overhang on the west side, providing a large sheltered space in this very wet climate. There is a 5-foot (1.5-meter) cantilevered overhang on the east side, and the trusses are laddered out for a four foot overhang on the north and south sides. Joe Zinni photo.

Fig. 4.60: Interior detail. Two six-by-twelve girders join over a post, and are bolted together. The heavy metal right-angle connector ties the girders to the post. All exposed metal is enameled black. Ceiling joists are supported by the girders and are joined together by going by each other over the girder, and then fastened together with one-half-inch bolts. Joe Zinni photo.

Fig. 4.61: Interior, during construction. Doubled eight-by-eight posts on left. Solid 16-by-16 posts on right. Doubled six-by-twelve girts on left. Single six-by-twelve girders on right. Six-by-twelve ceiling joists support the plank roof. This entire heavy-duty flat "landing pad" supports a truss system for the metal roofing. Joe Zinni photo.

Fig. 4.62: The Zinni's completed home, with cordwood infilling. The trusses have two different pitches on their top chords. Young Sage Zinni looks like a leprechaun next to this massive structure. Joe Zinni photo.

CHAPTER 5

Case Study: The Sunroom at Earthwood

I'VE BEEN PRACTICING "TIMBER FRAMING FOR THE REST OF US" SINCE 1975, but I never thought I'd write a book about it, so I wasn't careful about photographing the methods. When students at Earthwood said they really wanted a book on the subject, Jaki and I decided to build a second-story sunroom. We didn't really need the space, but figured that it would be a great photo opportunity for the book. Also, the ceiling was leaking in the room below the existing sitting deck and we needed a project for cordwood workshops, so we figured we had enough reasons build it. Now it's our favorite room, especially on sunny winter days.

With the book in mind, I deliberately used a variety of timber-framing techniques.

Design Overview of the Project

I have renovated old houses and started from scratch building new ones. Starting from scratch is easier.

We built a downstairs solar room within a year of Earthwood's completion in 1981. (Fig. 5.1). The room shared a common wall with the curved cordwood masonry wall of the home, the curvature flattened somewhat by a six-foot-wide (1.8-meter-wide) sliding glass door. The east and west walls feature cordwood, a door, and a small window. The long well-posted south wall is mostly thermalpane glass. A six-by-ten girder — or girt — supported the radial four-by-eight ceiling joist system which extended through the solar room. These joists also supported an outdoor sitting deck of two-by-six pressure-treated planking. Between the ceiling joists, we had installed corrugated fiberglass panels, gently sloped to the south. Rainwater dripping through the deck boards fell onto the panels and was carried away, where it dripped harmlessly onto a crushed stone walkway below. For insulation, we installed extruded polystyrene to the underside of the ceiling joists.

Fig. 5.1: This is how Earthwood looked for over 20 years, a sitting deck over the original downstairs solar room.

All of this worked fine for a few years, but mice found their way into the space over the insulation, as they are wont to do in the country, and, after a while, the corrugated fiberglass began to leak slightly. After twenty years, the insulation was smelly and in bad shape, a combination of mouse mess and moisture. Something had to be done, whether we built a new room over the top or not.

Jaki and I tore out the rigid insulation and the one-by boards that supported it, only to discover that the four-by-eight joists were in bad shape. One or two of them might have been saved, but we decided to replace the lot. The new ceiling joists would be left uncovered — insulation would not be necessary with a finished room upstairs — and we wanted the room to look nice. New tongue-in-groove planking might as well be supported by fresh-smelling and unstained ceiling joists. Building the new sunroom also meant reclaiming the old one, doubling the advantage of space gained.

Design Questions and Plans

We had several conversations about the use of the new space, where the door and windows would go, and the like. We agreed that we wanted plenty of south-facing windows and that they would have to be of some opening style with a screen option. We found some excellent Caradco™ double-hung windows at a good price, but what really sold Jaki on them was that both the upper and lower sashes could be rotated 180 degrees for easy cleaning. After all, there would be no easy access to the windows exterior on the second story.

A nagging question was whether or not we would be able to maintain the same 1:12 roof slope in an upstairs addition and still have sufficient headroom. I checked this with my tape measure and found that there would be plenty of headroom, even at the southern end of the extended five-by-ten roof rafters. We proceeded to the design stage.

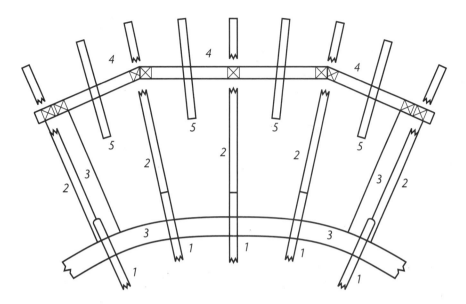

Fig. 5.2: New sunroom, post, girder, and rafter plan. The four short cantilevered rafters cut the long planking spans in half. This cantilever is made possible by the generous overhang.

Key:

1 Existing five-by-ten (12.7 cm-by-25.4 cm) radial rafters at Earthwood.

2 The sun room five-by-ten rafters extend the originals.

3 Cordwood walls, 16 inches (40.6 cm) thick.

4 Girts on south wall, all eight-by-tens (20.3 cm-by-25.4 cms).

5 Secondary double-cantilevered five-by-ten rafters.

X Post location.

Note: that two of the posts are resawn to make the angle.

Before tearing the pressure-treated boards off, I used a black crayon to lay out the new room on the outside deck, a great aid in planning. We could visualize and mark all the components in their actual positions. Then, on paper, and using a scale of one-half-inch to the foot, I drew the post-and-beam support structure (Fig. 5.2), and a second plan at the same scale, this one for the replacement four-by-eight system which would serve as the floor support for the new addition. (Fig. 5.3). Note that the primary difference between the upstairs rafter plan and the downstairs ceiling joist plan (apart from timber dimensions) is the way the two different structures support the long planking spans which occur as the extended radial rafters get further apart.

I also drew elevations of all three new sides of the new room, so that I could figure out the windows and door, as well as the post, height. Drawing the extended rafters in scale, and at the correct pitch, showed the post height, and these figures could be checked on site with actual measurements. (Figures 5.4, 5.5 and 5.6). I submitted my plans, along with the $15 fee, to the town's building inspector, and got a permit, an important step.

The plans also made it easy to generate a materials list, which, in April, I brought to two sawmills for bid. We accepted the slightly higher bid because of quicker and more reliable delivery. This gave the timbers more drying time, and the decision seems to have been a good one, as we have not experienced egregious

Fig. 5.3: The floor joists for the new room (which are also the ceiling joists for the old one) have four transverse headers to support one end of the short secondary joists. A self-supporting cantilever was not possible at this level in the way that it was for the roof rafters.

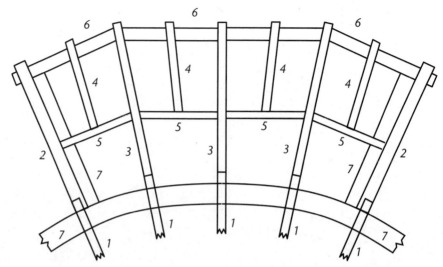

Key:

1 Existing four-by-eight (10.1 cm-by-20.3 mm) radial joists at Earthwood.

2 Eight-by-eight (20.3 cm-by-20.3 cm) cedar girts newly installed at top of existing cordwood wall.

3 Replacement four-by-eight joists, married to house joists.

4 Secondary four-by-eight joists cut planking span in half.

5 Headers, all four-by-eights.

6 South wall girts or girders, all eight-by-tens (20.3 cm-by-25.4 cms).

7 Cordwood walls, 16 inches (40.6 cm) thick. Cordwood walls under south-facing windows (see Fig. 5.6) are 8 inches (20.3 cm) thick.

Fig. 5.4: East elevation, with door.
Key:

1 Five-by-ten (12.7 cm-by-25.4 cm) rafter.

2 Eight-by-ten (20.3 m-by-25.4 cm) girt or girder.

3 Eight-by-eight (20.3 cm-by-20.3 m) post.

4 Eight-by-eight cedar girt.

5 Four-by-eight (10.1 cm-by-20.3 cm) doorframe.

6 Typical cordwood masonry infilling.

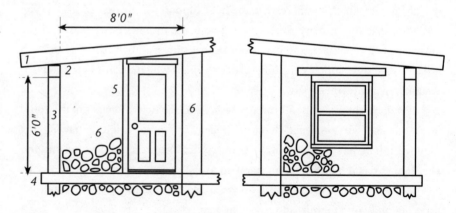

Fig. 5.5, above right: West elevation, with a heavily framed double-hung window "floating" in the cordwood masonry. Note window lintel, composed of two four-by-eights, side by side. See Fig. 5.4, above left, for framing details.

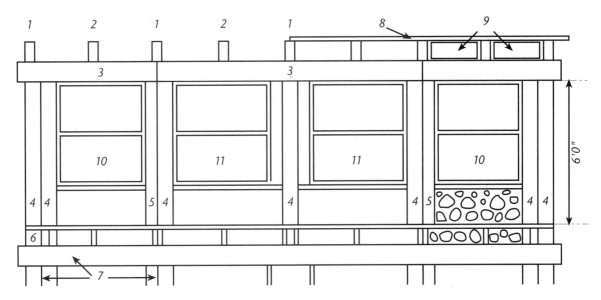

Key:

1 Primary five-by-ten (12.7 cm-by-25.4 cm) rafters

2 Secondary (short) five-by-ten rafters

3 Eight-by-ten (20.3 cm-by-25.4 cm) girts

4 Eight by eight (20.3 cm-by-20.3 cm) posts, six feet long

5 Six-by-eight (15.2 cm-by-20.3 cm) posts, cut at an angle to make the bend in the south wall (See Fig. 5.2)

6 Eight-by-eight cedar girt

7 Existing lower story framework

8 Two-by-six (3.8 cm-by-14.0 cm) tongue-and-groove planking

9 Eight-by-eight beam pieces as snowblocking

10 42-inch-wide by 48-inch-high (107cm by 122 cm) double-hung windows

11 46-inch-wide by 48-inch-high (117cm by 122cm) double-hung windows

Fig. 5.6: The South elevation plan was key in determining the height of posts — six feet (1.8 meters) — as well as their location with respect to the existing downstairs structure. "Snowblocking" between rafters consists of pieces of cedar eight-by-eights that I had on hand. Cordwood masonry is eight inches thick under the windows and as snowblocking between four-by-eight floor joists.

wood shrinkage. The heavy timbers, as listed, cost about $760. This list is given as an example only. Adjustments were made, so it may or may not serve as an accurate materials list to build a similar sunroom. The "purpose" column matters little to the sawyer, but will be helpful to you when you try to figure out what all these pieces are for.

The flooring and roofing two-by-six tongue-and-groove planks are not included. We needed about 850 board feet of these, which cost us $773.

Timber Schedule for Earthwood Sunroom

(all white pine except as noted)

Quantity	Dimensions	Length	Purpose
7	5" × 10" (12.7 × 25.4 cm)	10' (3 m)	Rafters (2 cut in half)
1	8" × 10" (20.3 × 25.4 cm)	12' (3.6 m)	Main (center) south wall girt
1	8" × 10" (20.3 × 25.4 cm)	14' (4.3 m)	Right and left south wall girts (cut into 2 @ 7').
4	8" × 8" (20.3 × 203 cm)	14' (4.3 m)	Posts (when cut in half)
1	6" × 8" (15.2 × 20.3 cm)	14' (4.3 m)	Posts (when cut in half)
7	4" × 8" (10.1 × 20.3 cm)	10' (3 m)	Floor joists (2 cut in half)
8	4" × 8" (10.1 × 20.3 cm)	8' (2.4 m)	Door frames (1 for lintel, 1 extra)
6	1" × 6" (2.5 × 15.2 cm)	8' (2.4 m)	Cordwood key pieces and other
4	1" × 10" (2.5 × 25.4 cm)	12' (3.6 m)	Broaden lower story girders
1	1" × 12" (2.5 × 30.5 cm)	10' (3 m)	Finish interior of lower story posts
2	2" × 8" (5.1 × 20.3 cm)	12' (3.6 m)	South wall window framing
(The following pieces shall be northern white cedar)			
2	8" × 8" (20.3 × 20.3 cm)	10" (3 m)	East and west downstairs wall girts
4	2" × 8" (5.1 × 20.3 cm)	8" (2.4 m)	West wall window framing

An eraser is one of your most valuable tools. Figure out the structure and jointing details on paper, ahead of time. Erasing and redrawing a few lines at the design stage can save major headaches later on. If you can't visualize the situation from paper plans, build a scale model, a great way to figure out how things are connected. If you can't build the model, maybe you shouldn't try to build the real thing.

I have deliberately described the order of events we followed, because it is typical of any building project, large or small. It all starts with conceptualization of the project, which should involve all of the interested parties. This is followed by more detailed drawings, securing a building permit, and, finally, the pricing and procurement of materials. After all that is done…

Work Begins

Former Earthwood student Doug Kerr visited for a week to help out on the early stages of the project. He wanted to learn timber framing, but didn't want to wait for the book. Doug arrived in the evening, and the next

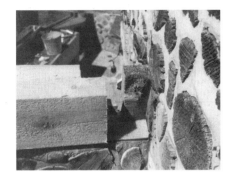

morning we tore up the entire front sitting deck, and all of the original four-by-eight deck joists. The post-and-beam frame of the original solar room's south wall was still in excellent condition.

The east and west walls of the lower story were 16-inch cordwood walls, and, for insulation and architectural purposes, we wanted to maintain that same width and style in the new addition. I chose to install new cedar eight-by-eight girts where the old deteriorated doubled four-by-eights had been removed. The south end of the eight-by-eight would be supported directly by the six-by-ten girder that ran along the south side of the original solar room. But how would we fasten the northern ends of these girts? Improvisation. There was enough of a stub on each of the original four-by-eight floor joists to fasten to, as seen in Fig. 5.7. With my

chainsaw, I removed a 4- by 4-inch by 8-inch-high (10.1- by 10.1-centimeter by 20.3-centimeter-high) chunk of wood from the new cedar girt, and fastened it to the stub using two seven-inch (180-millimeter) lag screws. Remember that the cordwood wall would also be supporting this girt all along its length. Fig. 5.8 shows the east wall girt being installed.

Extending Floor Joists

We used two different methods of joining the new four-by-eight floor joists to the original floor joists, because we were faced with two different

Fig. 5.7: I notched the east side eight-by-eight girt to fit it up against the stub of the original four-by-eight rafter. I chiseled and scraped deteriorated wood, back to sound material, and doused the area with a water-sealing product. Note the use of Sill Seal™ between the girt and the top mortar joint of the cordwood wall.

Fig. 5.8: We install the east side girt.

Fig. 5.9: Glue is applied to the gusset.

Fig. 5.10: Gussets are screwed and glued to the joists, with half of the gusset on each side of the join.

Fig. 5.11: Doug tightens a hex nut up to a washer on the threaded end of one of the bolts. As Doug looks at the stub, he is installing a bolt at the upper left and lower right of the stub, keeping about three inches from all edges. The carriage end of the bolt is on the other side of the unit, and is drawn into the new four-by-eight by tightening the nut. We countersunk the nuts and washers, so that we could use 8-inch bolts without the threaded end protruding from the joist.

situations. The center floor joist had only 6½ inches (16.5 centimeters) of good sound four-by-eight extending from the wall. As it was the center joist, maintaining symmetry was important. In this case, we used a wooden gusset system, the gussets made from two scrap pieces of two-by-eight material, each about a foot long. In Fig. 5.9, I apply wood glue to one side of one of the gussets. In many instances, gussets are made of plywood, such as with homemade trusses. I didn't have plywood at the ready in this case, and, as the join would be exposed, I figured that the two-by-eight pieces would look better anyway. Gussets used in this fashion must be used in pairs, one each side of the joint, just like truss plates on trusses. Otherwise, most of the strength of the joint is lost.

In Fig. 5.10, I used an electric drill to mount the glued gusset to the two four-by-eights which are butted together. I used four screws on each side of the joint. Half of the gusset (six inches or 15.2 centimeters) was screwed and glued to the original stub, and the other half was similarly fastened to the new joist. The gusset on the other side got the same treatment.

The remaining two joist extensions were a different situation, so we used a different solution. The original joists extended into the space about eighteen inches (45.7 centimeters), and symmetry was not an issue, the way it was in the center. So in this case, we simply fastened the new four-by-eight alongside of the original member, using glue and two strong one-half-inch by 8-inch (1.2- by 20.0-centimeter) carriage bolts. Carriage bolts have rounded heads and a square section just under the head that grabs the wood by pressure and friction. The trick here is to join the rafters together temporarily while a half-inch hole is drilled all the way through both. There are a variety of clamps that will work for this purpose, or you can temporarily toe-screw the two pieces together while you drill. Again, glue between the pieces makes for a stronger joint. In our case, I used just two large bolts to make the joint. See Fig. 5.11.

Fig. 5.12: The author toe-screws the four-by-eight joist to the six-by-ten girder.

Fastening the Joist to the Girder

The nice thing about wide joists like four-by-eights and five-by-tens is that they are stable when supported by a wall or girder, unlike two-bys, which can fall over quite easily. Cross-bracing or bridging of two-bys is not only prudent, but building codes require it. Another nice thing about heavy joists is that they are esthetically pleasing, particularly when the depth of the timber is twice as great as its breadth.

Fiig. 5.13: A right angle fastener can take the place of toenails or toe-screws.

Four-by-eights are very stable over the girder, but they must still be fastened, so that they don't slide laterally. In Fig. 5.12, I am toe-screwing the joist to the six-by-ten girder. In Fig. 5.13, I use a right-angle galvanized plate to hold the joist in its correct position over the girder.

Installing Headers

A header is a short transverse wooden member used to provide support for an otherwise unsupported joist or rafter. An example is when a roof rafter needs to be cut to make way for a skylight; a header spans between the adjacent rafters to frame the skylight.

The floor joist system for our new room required headers for a different reason. As the radial floor joists get further from the center of the house, they also get

Fig. 5.14: We made ten of these little support pieces very quickly.

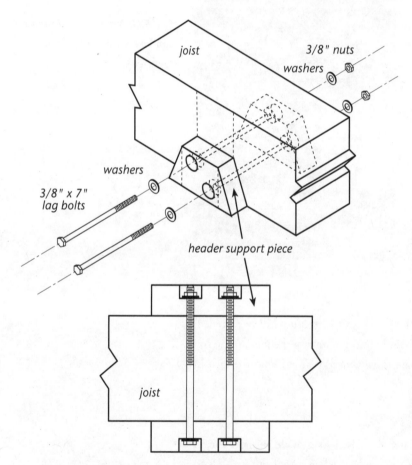

Fig. 5.15: The locations of the header, the header support piece, and the drill holes are all marked on the four-by-eight floor/ceiling joist. We actually used carriage bolts, but countersunk lag bolts could be used as well.

Drawing by Doug Kerr.

further apart from each other. This increases planking spans until we begin to experience a "springy" floor (deflection), an indication that planking span is being stretched too far.

The simple solution would have been to run another radial floor joist halfway between the primary ones, cutting all planking spans in half. The problem was that there was an existing cordwood wall, which would have needed rebuilding to make room for one end of the new joists; a lot of work. Besides, planking spans were okay near the round house; they only started to get dicey a few feet away from the main building.

Four headers, as shown in Fig. 5.3, enabled us to support one end of a shorter secondary rafter. The existing girder would support its outermost end. There are two easy ways to fasten the headers: The first is to use metal joist hangers made for the purpose. But we didn't want to see the galvanized hangers, and besides, our local supplier did not carry them for full-sized four-bys. The second is to use two strong lag bolts — say one-half-inch by eight inches — installed through the side of a joist and into the end grain of the header. Place them about two inches from the top and two inches from the bottom of the members, and centered on the width of the header. This was an attractive idea, but once one header was installed, it would not be possible to install the next one in the same way — not if I wanted to maintain the symmetry of Fig. 5.3. I thought of offsetting each header by four inches, so that the lag screws could always be driven in, but this spoiled the symmetry and I would still have a problem getting lag screws into the headers where they meet the east and west cordwood walls.

Once again, improvisation saved the day. I came up with a header support system that was attractive (it was made of wood), strong, and could be assembly-lined quite easily. I made ten little trapezoidal header support pieces from a standard two-by-four, each with a base of seven inches (17.8 centimeters) and a top dimension of four inches (10.1 centimeters) to match the four-by-eight headers. I simply marked the two-by-four with my square and made all the cuts quickly with a circular saw. I made ten of the little guys while I was at it, even though only eight were required, in case I spoiled one or two. Fig. 5.14 shows one of the support pieces and a couple of three-eighths-inch by seven-inch carriage bolts, used as fasteners.

On the joists, using a square and pencil, I marked the intended locations where the headers would join in. Using one of my trapezoids as a template, I drew its final position as well, and the location of two carriage bolts that would hold everything together. See Fig. 5.15.

It would have been difficult to hold the two trapezoids in place (one on each side of the joist) while drilling two 7-inch-long holes through all of the pieces, so Doug and I decided to drill just the joist itself with a three-eights-inch bit — that was easy — and then hold the individual trapezoid supports in place and mark their hole locations with either a pencil or by a quick tickle with the tip of the drill. This was a nice two-person job.

Once the two supports were marked, we took them down and finished the holes, being careful to drill as straight as possible. On one of the supports, we used a one-inch spade bit to put a countersink on the outside for the washer and nut. We didn't want hardware in the way of installing the headers.

Installation of the header supports was now easy. We glued one side of each piece and inserted the carriage bolt from the non-glued side. Fig. 5.16. This assembly was installed on the joist by tapping the bolts through the three-eights-inch holes. Then the other trapezoid support was installed, glued side against the joist, and the washers and nuts were made fast in the countersink. See Fig. 5.17. The carriage end of the bolt is drawn into the two-by-four, where it will be out of the way of header installation later on.

Fig. 5.16, near right: The supports are glued and the carriage bolts installed.

Fig. 5.17, far right: Doug tightens the hex nut, completing the header support installation.

Fig. 5.18, below: Doug places the header onto its supports.

With the supports in place, we'd run slightly long four-by-eight header stock over the top of the joists where it would connect and mark its underside with a pencil. This eliminated measuring. Using patterns is generally superior to measuring and trying to figure angles. We cut the headers to length with a chainsaw and tried them in place. A good idea in any operation like this is to always do the longest piece first. If you make a bad cut, you get to re-cut it and use it at a shorter location. If you spoil the shortest one first, you don't get a second chance. ("Dagnabbit it! I've cut this piece three times and it's still too short!" — Old carpenter's joke.)

If the piece fits, now is the time to cut notches out of each end so that it bears on the header supports. These notches will be 3½ inches (8.9 centimeters) high and 1½ inches (3.8 centimeters) wide, matching a common store-bought two-by-four stud. If it fits the first time, congratulations! Chances are, though, that you may have to take the piece down and scrape or trim a little to make it fit. Trying and fitting is all part of any kind of timber framing. See Fig. 5.18.

Finally, a couple of toenails — from the top, out of sight — will keep the header from wandering.

Installing the Secondary Joists

With the headers installed, we can now fasten the secondary joists, the shorter ones whose purpose is to cut the planking span in half. Cut one end square, where it will abut the header, and let the other end run long. Always let rough-cut joists and rafters run long on the outside, so that you can snap a chalk-line later and cut them all at one time, all the right length for the overhang. If you cut them the length you think they should be, Mr. Murphy's famous law will almost guarantee that you'll wish you hadn't. Chalk-lines are like patterns: they are always superior to measuring.

Fig. 5.19: The floor frame for the new room is completed, and the first two flooring planks are installed.

Now is the time to use the simple fastening method alluded to in the previous section. We marked the location of the joist on the header and drilled two seven-sixteenths-inch holes through the wood so that lag screws would meet the end-grain of the joist about two inches from the top and two inches from the bottom—centered right and left, of course. Have someone hold the joist temporarily in place while you tickle its squared end with the drill. Take it down and continue the holes — straight, please — into the end grain of the joist, as deep as is needed for the lag screw used. With a one-half-inch by seven-inch lag screw — plenty strong for the purpose — drill your hole about 2¾ (7.0 centimeters) inches into the joist. Put a washer under the hex-head of the lag screw and install the bolt. An assistant may have to resist from the other end, to prevent a space occurring between the two members.

Mark and fasten the joist to the girder using one of the methods shown in Figs. 5.12 and 5.13.

The completed floor framework is shown in Fig. 5.19.

Fig. 5.20: Doug draws the new board tight with a long spike, which has had its point driven a little ways into the joist. The spike is now a class 2 lever with tremendous mechanical advantage for drawing tongue-in-groove boards together. Start the nail first.

Flooring (Decking)

We decided on two-by-six V-jointed tongue-and-groove spruce planking for our floor. The V-jointed side goes down, making an attractive ceiling as seen from the room below. We like it for its strength, appearance, and ease of installation. We also like the benefit of doing the floor and ceiling below in one operation, a real plus with the plank-and-beam system. Also, we wanted to maintain visual consistency with the original floor, because there would be a direct doorway opening from the dining room into the new sunroom.

The toughest part of the planking was installing the first board, because it had to be scribed to fit a very rough-textured cordwood masonry wall, as can be seen in Fig. 5.19. Fortunately, the round house was slightly flattened at this point because of a six-foot wide sliding glass door unit below. Still, the first plank had to be scribed with a pencil and cut to fit up against the cordwood wall without huge gaps. I used chisels and a variety of saws to trim the edge that went up against the cordwood wall, the edge with the tongue on it. With new work, especially with conventional rectilinear construction, you will not have this sort of problem. Again, starting from scratch is easier.

Once the first plank was installed, the rest went quite easily. You could hire a machine for blind-nailing tongue-and-groove planking, but I have always used cup-headed nails to attach the planks. These nails can be driven slightly below the surface, so that the floor can be sanded prior to finishing. Use two nails at each place where the plank is supported by a joist, with the nails about an inch inward from both the end of the board and the edge. I insert the tongue of one board into the groove of the board already nailed, then use a ten-inch log cabin spike to draw the tongue absolutely tight into the groove, leaving no space between boards on the top surface. (Remember that the underside has that attractive V-joint, so the boards can only be laid with the non-jointed side up.) While holding the pressure with one hand, I drive the two nails in with the other. You might find it easier to start the nails before drawing the boards up snug. See Fig. 5.20.

With rectilinear buildings, you will want to design the building to maximize the use of the boards. The boards I was able to purchase came only in 12- and 16-

foot lengths. Our floor sections were trapezoidal in shape, so, with our ever-increasing planking span, scrap pieces would constantly get shorter. On subsequent sections, we used the scrap pieces in the reverse order in which they were created. We waited until the first large central section (or facet) was about half covered before cutting the ends. We snapped a chalk-line down the edge of the section, centered over the middle of the four-by-eight joist below. Then I set my circular saw's blade so that it cut just a little bit deeper than the thickness of the planking, by about one-sixteenth inch (1.6 millimeters). Now I could cut a fair bit of the section at once, and get a nice straight line.

Fig. 5.21: The chalk-line has been snapped, and I cut the ends of all of the boards in this section at once. If done in the middle of a four-by-eight joist, this will leave a two-inch-wide bearing surface for the next facet. At the edge of the building, a straight overhang can be created in this way.

Fig. 5.22: All the important structural members are marked on the deck with a black marker.

On subsequent facets, it is necessary to trim one end of the board to the proper angle in order to fit it up to the previous section. Use an adjustable angle square to measure and mark this angle. Again, let the extra length of the plank run long, so that all the ends can be trimmed at once. We did this upstairs on the roof planking, and the extra length of the board became the overhang, which was all trimmed at once by a single straight cut with the saw. See Fig. 5.21.

Doug Kerr and I tore out the old deck and joists, installed the new joists, and decked the whole area in just four days, not bad for renovation work. Thanks, Doug!

Preparing the Girders

Once the floor was complete, I transposed the plans onto the deck with a black marker, at full scale. Now the position of every post could be seen clearly on the deck, and I could even show how the major south wall girders could abut with each other over the posts. See Fig. 5.22. I could check with the structure below to make sure that the line of thrust was transferred directly on compression to the post below, and not just missing them, as per Fig. 2.9 on page 24.

Before installing the posts, my family and I laid the girders out on the deck, supported on little blocks of wood. Then, the corresponding ends of the girders were cut at an angle so that they joined together fairly well. This was done by marking with a pencil and with judicious use of both an angle square and a regular framing square. Each piece was cut with a chainsaw. Now the girders were repositioned on the little blocks of wood, as in Fig. 5.23 and Fig. 5.24.

Unless one is a very skilled chainsaw carpenter, the chances are that the butt join between the two girders won't be all that great. Good, possibly, but not great. You can make it great by butting the two girders together as closely as possible, and then passing the chainsaw down between them, as in Fig. 5.24. Helpers can lend their weight to the project,

Fig. 5.23: The girders are mocked up on the deck.

Fig. 5.24: Passing a chainsaw down through the joint, maybe more than once, will eventually give a pretty good fit. Make sure the chain is sharp. If you shorten the central girder by a half-inch or so, thats okay. There is plenty of space on top of an eight-by-eight post. Let the shorter girders run long. They can be trimmed later.

one on each girder. You may have to do this two or three times, butting the girders again after each cut. Pretty soon, you'll have a great butt joint, and this joint will be ready for use when the girders are assembled permanently on top of the six-foot-high (1.8-meter-high) posts. It is just much easier to get these girders to match up well on the deck, than to do the work overhead. Be wary of chainsaw "kickback," both while cutting and when the saw completes the cut.

Installing Posts

From the plan, we know that the posts should be six feet (1.8 meters) long. With the eight-by-ten girders on top of them, this gives six foot ten inches of clearance to the underside of the rafters at the lowest point. And it is seven foot eight inches to the ceiling, so there is a cozy, but not oppressive, feeling of space in the room. The rafter clearance is a few inches greater near the house.

Jaki and I were joined by family and interested friends for the remainder of the framing and roofing projects, including sons Darin and Rohan, Anna Milburn-Lauer, Bruce Kilgore, Diane Lukaris, and Stephanie Bayan. Work became fun with this rotating crew, a huge advantage.

I cut eight-by-eights with a chainsaw. The saw needs to be well sharpened, which means that it must not only cut easy, but also true, without pulling one way. The very best way to assure straight cutting is to use a new bar and new chain. The next best way is to use a chain which has been professionally sharpened with a machine for the purpose. In any case, don't make your first cut on an important short post. If you mess it up, the post may be rendered useless. Practice your technique on a long eight-by-eight, and keep cutting two inches (5.1 centimeters) off it until you can do a good job with regularity. Finally, when you've got a good square right-angled cut, and your confidence is high, measure, mark and cut the other end to length.

Bruce Kilgore made a wonderful cordwood cutoff saw, for use in making very regular log-ends for his house. He loaned me the saw, and I used it to cut quite a few of the heavy timbers for our sunroom frame. An explanation of how to make this saw is shown at pages 74–77 of my previous book *Cordwood Building: The State of the Art* (see Bibliography). A saw like this affords great control options. The swing of the saw can be fine-tuned to give a vertical cut every time. If need be, a shingle can be installed as a shim against the backrest of the table, giving another opportunity for fine angle adjustments. See pages 124–125.

No matter what method of cutting you choose, the cut may need to be dressed a little if it is still not square. Check it again with the large framing square and mark any high bits on the cut with a pencil. A little extra wood can be removed easily with a small Stanley Sure-Form™ Scraper, which has a 2- by 2½-inch (5.1- by 6.3-centimeter) rasp on one end, and a handle that is used to pull the rasp towards you. You can put a lot of pressure on the wood with this tool, and it can remove wood very quickly. Another tool I use for the same purpose is my 5"-diameter Makita 4000-rpm circular sander, with #36-grit sanding disks for heavy wood removal, and #80 grit for finer work. Hint: very often, removing a high spot at the center of the new cut will stop a post from wobbling. Let the post bear on the edges.

Frequent use of the square and pencil is imperative, and becomes habitual after a while. With hand-hewn beams, or a timber with considerable wane on the edge, you may want to run a straightedge along the surface of the beam, and use your square off of the straightedge.

There Are All Kinds of Ways to Cut a Beam

Chainsaw

Fig. 5.25: Chainsaw.

The author cuts a heavy timber supported at a convenient height by sawhorses. The saw cut can be no better than:

1. The accuracy with which the pencil marks are transposed to the timber. Use a good carpenter's square and mark all around the timber, to make sure that — after its circumnavigation — the mark returns to the point of beginning. If it doesn't, the cut cannot be square. Always set your square on the beam being cut, not on the piece being cut off.

2. The quality of the chain and bar. The right- and left-side chain teeth must be sharpened equally to prevent pull to either direction, and the bar must be straight, with a clean, un-nicked groove.

3. The skill of the operator. In this regard, I can only say: Practice, practice, practice! Always cut on the long side of the line. A chainsaw removes about a quarter inch of wood. This is called the kerf. Don't make your post a quarter inch short!

Note the use of a chainsaw safety helmet for sound and kickback protection, as well as to keep wood chips out of your eyes. Use protective leg chaps in case the saw cuts through the timber and continues on to your knees and legs.

Cutoff saw

Fig. 5.26 Cutoff saw.

This cutoff saw moves the chain through a vertical arc, perpendicular to the timber on the table. This advantage makes it easier to maintain a consistently straight cut.

There are also 24-inch circular saws made for crosscutting, also called beam cutters or compound miter saws. Log cabin builders and professional timber framers use these all the time. Contractor Russell Pray owns one of these and used it to make perfect right-angle cuts on the posts and beams at the Earthwood garage. They are very expensive, though, and it would make more economic sense to hire one for a day from a contractor's tool rental store rather than buy one.

The following option is much more affordable.

Crosscut saw attachment for a circular saw

Fig. 5.27. The Prazi Beam Cutter.
Photo supplied by Prazi USA.

A great new development in crosscutting is the Linear Link™ power saw from Muskegon Power Tool (see Appendix C for contact information for Muskegon and also for Prazi, a manufacturer of a similar tool, the Beam Cutter™.) The tool combines the best features of a chainsaw and a circular saw, allowing straight cuts up to 12 inches (30.5 centimeters) deep on vertical cuts, and well over 8 inches (20.3 centimeters) deep on a 45-degree angle cut. You can buy the complete unit for about $540 (March 2003) or, for about $220, you can buy a conversion kit for your Skil™ or Craftsman™ worm drive circular saws. (The $130 Prazi unit will fit Makita and DeWalt "sidewinders" as well.)

This sturdy chain kit can replace your circular saw blade in a few minutes, and enables you to make deep accurate crosscuts through beams up to a foot thick. Think of the accuracy and convenience of a circular saw, combined with the depth of a chainsaw. It can even be used to do minor "saw milling," if you need to rip an inch or two off the edge of a beam. (For major saw milling, use one of the chainsaw mills described in Chapter 3.)

Circular saw and handsaw

Fig. 5.28: Circular saw and handsaw.

After marking the square cut all the way around with a pencil and square, use a circular saw to cut as deeply as possible into all four surfaces, all the way around the beam and back to the original side. My seven-inch (17.8-centimeter) circular saw will allow me to make a vertical cut 2-1/2 inches (6.3 centimeters) deep, maximum. With an eight-by-eight, cutting into all four surfaces will leave a square of uncut wood in the center about three inches (7.6 centimeters) square, which you can finish with a good sharp handsaw. The cuts made with the circular saw will guide your handsaw straight through.

Fig. 5.29: Jaki and Anna plumb a post.

Fig. 5.30: The author toe-screws the base of the post to the floor.

When you think you've got a good square base on your post, try it at its actual location to see if it stands up vertically. If it is good, measure (twice!) and make the square cut at the top end. Don't be nervous — timber framing for the rest of us is quite forgiving, unless you happen to be a card-carrying obsessive-compulsive neat freak. Tapered cedar shingles will tighten up any joint, and can often be hidden, or at least sanded smooth and rendered almost invisible.

Once the post is the right length, stand it in place. Fastening to concrete foundations was discussed in Chapter 4. In our sunroom, we were standing the post onto a wooden substrate, the two-by-six tongue-and-groove floor.

In Fig. 5.29 Jaki and Anna plumb a post. We felt we had a good square cut on this one, yet it still wanted to lean in slightly. Anna tapped in the thin edge of an eight-inch-wide cedar shingle, while Jaki consulted the plumb bubble of her four-foot level. In Fig. 5.30, I toe-screw the post in place, a couple of screws each side. Right angle connectors are another option here.

Because of the odd angles where girders meet on the south wall (please revisit Fig. 5.2), two of the posts required some custom work at the sawmill. I used my angle square to capture this angle, and transposed it to the ends of a couple of six-by-eight posts, already made. I took the timbers back to the sawmill and showed Norm, the sawyer, how the post needed to be ripped on the bias so that, when placed up against its neighbor, the resulting "double-wide" post makes the slight angle turn in the wall. Norm loves this sort of challenge, and clamped the piece onto his movable carriage with shims to create the angle. In no time, I had the required posts with their trapezoidal cross-sections.

Installing the Girders

The posts are all installed — and braced — and the girders have had their angles cut as described above (see Preparing the Girders, pages 121–122). Now it is time to blow the whistle on some muscle and heft the girders into place. We had enough help right in the family so that I could hide behind the camera. By the way, I think of these beams as girders, because they support rafters, but, as they are on the edge of a building, they can also be called girts.

Fig. 5.31: Sons Rohan (right) and Darin (left) lift the ends up onto the tops of the double-wide posts, while Jaki and Anna lighten their load with assistance from below.

We started with the west girder, letting the west end run long. Its overhang could be cut to length later in situ. We did not fasten it yet, for its own weight kept it in place. The second one — the central girder — was the really heavy one: a ten-foot six-inch full-sized eight-by-ten of fairly green white pine. But many hands make light work. See Fig. 5.31.

After all three girders were set in place, we adjusted their positions slightly with a heavy hammer, sliding them this way and that until we were happy with the way they sat and joined each other. Small wooden shingle shims can be used as necessary to take any wobbles out. Then I toe-screwed up through the posts into the underside of the girders, using two screws at each side of a post. Fig. 5.32. I made a mistake at this point that you can avoid. I should have fastened the top sides of the girders together with truss plates, as I had done many times

before. I either forgot to do this, or felt it wasn't necessary, or thought that the truss plates might get in the way of rafters later on; I really don't remember. (And excuses are like belly buttons; everybody has one.)

But the girders did separate by about a quarter inch (6.3 millimeters) later on. This is a cosmetic — as opposed

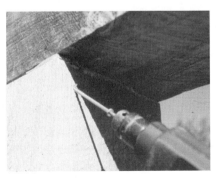

Fig. 5.32: A couple of screws hold the girder in place. Right-angle connectors are good in this situation, too.

Raising Heavy Timbers

Traditional timber framers will make all their bents ahead of time, and have them stacked in the proper order, waiting for the big day when plenty of help is gathered together for the raising. Lots of bodies wielding poles, as seen in Fig. 2.17, lift the bent to vertical. The poles can also act as temporary stops to aid during the lifting process. Someone — usually the boss — checks the bent for plumb, as diagonal bracing is fastened.

Oftentimes, professional timber framing contractors hire a crane for the big day.

My experience over thirty years has been to raise posts individually, brace them with temporary diagonal supports, and then to raise the girts or girders one at a time. Usually, this involves just two to four people, as at the Earthwood addition, but, in the case of a 30-foot ten-by-ten at Log End Cave, eight people and a pick-up truck were involved in the installation.

Mark Powers, now building a Log End Cave type of home with very heavy rafters, and working mostly alone, says: "With some creative engineering, I've been able to raise all of my girders and rafters with my trusty Kubota 45-horsepower tractor with its quick-attach forks and bucket. I can't imagine building the house without it."

At Earthwood, I had fun raising a fairly green 15-foot ten-by-twelve oak girder — probably over 700 pounds (318 kilos) in weight — to the top of the posts, aided by just one other helper. We accomplished the feat by raising an end of the timber with a lever, and slipping a concrete block under it, about 40 percent of the way along its length. Now lifting the other end was easy, as the overhanging 40 percent of the beam's weight cancelled out another 40 percent of the weight at the lifting end. Again, we made a slightly higher block stack 40 percent of the way in from the new lifting end. We alternated our lifts back and forth, end to end, always adding a block or two to the low stack. After a couple of lifts, we rebuilt the block stack with criss-crossed block construction, for greater safety and stability. In short order, we had the beam up to height, and then, one end at a time, transferred its load onto the braced posts.

to structural — problem, and it could easily have been avoided. But as I have said before, heavy timber framing is forgiving, particularly if you are willing to forgive yourself once in a while.

Installing the Five-by-Ten Rafters

As with the four-by-eight floor joists, we used two different methods of extending the five-by-ten radial roof rafters. The existing rafters, protected by a good overhang, were in excellent condition and extended between 18 and 23 inches (45.7 and 58.4 centimeters) from the cordwood walls. On the east and west rafters (which eventually would have supporting cordwood walls below them), we left the original overhanging rafters as they were, but cut a 2-by-10 by 22-inch (5.1-by-

25.4 by 55.9-centimeter) piece out of the new rafters so that they could fit up to the side of the overhanging rafters, as seen in Fig. 5.33. Then we used four one-half- by eight-inch lag bolts to hang the new rafter onto the old. The hex-heads and washers show on the outside. Carriage bolts are an option here.

Notice, in Fig. 5.33, that the original red pine rafter twisted slightly after construction, as red pine is inclined to do. I was able to straighten the rafter extension by making a biased cut out of the new rafter. This made for a tricky

Fig. 5.33: Rohan Roy tightens the nuts onto the lag bolts. Four one-half-inch lag bolts are plenty strong enough to make this joint.

chainsaw cut. The key to success in this sort of thing is to mark the angle correctly on the piece to be cut. And the key to marking it correctly is to double- and triple-check your angles and measurements. As I tend towards a slight dyslexia on this sort of thing, I would explain what I was doing to willing ears such as Rohan's. He picks up quickly on wooly-minded thinking.

After the framing was completed, and the roof installed, we covered this rather unattractive join with cordwood masonry. The outside looks great, as if it's a single rafter originating from the center of the house. On the inside, no rafter is in evidence, as it is hidden behind short log-ends.

The other three rafter extensions would be exposed in the room, so appearance was important. I designed a rafter plate which could be made from standard one-quarter- by 8-inch (.63- by 20.3-centimeter) steel stock. A twelve-foot section of this material was cut at the local Steel Service Center into six 24-inch (61 centimeter) pieces. I made a hole-drilling pattern out of a piece of plywood, and my friend Bruce Kilgore kindly drilled all the one-half-inch holes for me with his drill press. Before installation, Anna Milburn-Lauer painted all six pieces with two coats of spray-on flat black enamel.

As already stated, truss plates must be used on both sides of the joint for strength. Now, you may be tempted to try to fasten both plates to the rafter by the use of six-inch lag bolts, but leave that temptation behind. The chances of the holes of both plates lining up with holes drilled through the rafter are slim to nil. I saw

an architect-designed detail like this on a job once, where eight-by-eight posts were supposed to be installed into pre-drilled heavy metal U-shaped post holders, already fastened to the foundation. The architect wanted bolts all the way through, but the contractors couldn't hit the hole in the plate on the other side, even with their long bits. Lag screws from each side, however, are plenty strong, and that's what we chose.

Each plate would require eight half-inch by 3½-inch (1.2- by 9.0-centimeter) hex-headed lag screws. Six

Fig. 5.34: Anna tightens lag screws up against the metal plate, which acts as its own washer. Rohan drills three-eights-inch holes for the plate on the other side, appropriate for one-half-inch lag screws. He hangs the plate in position on two small screws, which hold it in place while he drills his holes. Fig. 5.45 on page 138 shows the completed detail

times eight is 48. It was quite a bit cheaper to buy two boxes with 25 screws per box than to buy 48 pieces out of the bin. So I have two left over.

The new rafter was butted up to the old rafter, with its south end supported by the new girder system, just installed. We jammed a two-by-four under the north end of the new rafter to hold it firmly against the end of the overhanging old rafter. Rohan and Anna installed the plates, as seen in Fig. 5.34.

"Balance-Beam" Secondary Rafters

We had the same deck situation upstairs as downstairs: planking span was starting to get rather extreme about six feet from the main building. But, this time, we could use a simple and rather elegant solution not available downstairs: short secondary rafters. They are, I suppose, a kind of double cantilever, but I think the term "balance beam" paints a more accurate picture. Have a peek, again, at the rafter plan, Fig. 5.2 on page 109. The four five-foot-long (1.5-meter-long) secondary rafters are supported at their middle by the eight-inch wide girder, with 26 inches (66 centimeters) extending out as overhang, and the other 26 inches extending in as … "underhang?" Whatever you call it, once the planking and heavy roofing is on, these short rafters are perfectly balanced, and their five- by ten-inch dimensions are stout enough to resist the shear and bending stresses of even a very heavy earth roof.

Anna and I installed them in a couple of hours. We'd already progressed with the roof planking beyond the point where the balance beams would go, which helped greatly with their installation. We simply manhandled (and woman-handled) the balance beams up into position, halfway between their longer brothers, and shimmed with shingles until the inner end of the beam was tight against the planking. This can be seen very clearly in Fig. 5.35.

When the room was completed, Jaki "suggested" that I cut a little 45-degree bevel into the rather stark exposed inner right angle of the rafters. I put up a little resistance — circular saw cuts overhead are not my favorite — but her idea is really a great design detail. A picture of this, Fig. 5.44, appears at the end of this chapter.

Fig. 5.35: The author checks the rafter position against pencil lines, while tapping in a couple of cedar shingles to snug it in place. Note the wooden straightedge outside the building, to assure that planking will hit all three rafters in a single flat plane. Anna Milburn-Lauer photo.

Planking the Roof

We used the same spruce two-by-six tongue-and-groove boards for the roof deck (sunroom ceiling) as we used for the floor. The most difficult part was tearing up a couple of feet of the earth roof on the house, so that we could marry the new roof to the old. I was pleased that the new material — from Russia — was almost identical to the lumber I'd used in the original roof, which was from Quebec. So, once the rafters had been extended, and the old gutter and drip edge removed, Anna and I were able to install the roof deck very quickly indeed, about two days. The work was easier than the floor because 1) we didn't have to fit the first plank to a cordwood wall, 2) there were only two — large — facets instead of three smaller ones, 3) we were nailing to five-by-eights instead of four-by-tens and 4) we could let all the boards run long and trim the east and west overhangs with one single straight cut. With regard to 4), I let the tongue-and-groove planks overhang eight inches on the east and west walls. More would have been nice, but I was concerned about going too far out with cantilevered planking, considering that the earth roof, soaking wet with snow, can weigh 185 pounds per square foot (903 kilos per square meter).

Fig. 5.36: The author makes a drip edge by bending two inches of a seven-inch-wide piece of flashing over the edge of the south overhang.

The Earth Roof

In the previous chapter, I told of the double-roof system, with false or secondary rafters over the real ones, and insulation as the filling of a plank sandwich. But the new sunroom extends the shallow 1:12 slope of the main house, and we wanted to continue out with the earth roof.

If plank-and-beam is my favorite structural system for roofs, then earth is my favorite roofing material. It is quiet and cool, warm and natural, cheap and beautiful, and ecologically harmonious. Done properly, it is also the longest-lasting roof, because the earth protects the substrate from the three things that break down every other roof surface: ultraviolet solar radiation, freeze-thaw cycling, and erosion.

While I have tried hard not to stray far from the subject of alternative timber framing in this book, I am going to make an exception here and devote a little space to the earth roof, because this information is so hard to find elsewhere, and I think earth roofs should be used wherever possible for the reasons given.

The best way to install an earth roof, in my view, is as follows:

1. Begin with a drip edge all around the building. You can buy ten-foot sections of galvanized metal drip edge for about $4 a section, but I prefer to make my own from seven-inch-wide aluminum flashing, so that I can place a full five inches onto the deck, which makes it easier to apply the membrane, and to keep it from the sun's UV rays. Fig. 5.36.

2. Install a good-quality waterproofing over the planking. I like the W.R. Grace Bituthene™ 4000 waterproofing membrane, because it is good quality, moderate in cost, and easy to install. Fig. 5.37.

3. Over the membrane, install four to six inches (10.1 to 15.2 centimeters) of extruded polystyrene insulation, rated at about R5 per inch. Fig. 5.38.

4. Over the insulation, place a continuous layer of 6-mil black polyethylene. This cheap black plastic (you can do a 1,000 square-foot, or 93 square-meter, roof for $60) is the base of the important drainage layer, which takes some burden off of the membrane. My earth-sheltered workshop

Fig. 5.37: Diane Lukaris and Jaki Roy roll out the Bituthene™ 4000 waterproofing membrane onto the wooden substrate, which has already been primed with a compatible acrylic primer provided with the product. The backing paper is removed as the 36-inch- wide membrane is rolled out, exposing a very sticky bitumastic membrane that adheres extremely well to the primed wooden deck. The ladies are careful to maintain the required three-inch overlap between adjacent courses.

Fig. 5.38: We installed 4 inches of Dow Styrofoam™, an extruded polystyrene, over the membrane.

students know that my favorite mantra in this regard is: "Drainage is the better part of waterproofing. Give water an easier place to go than into your house." Photos are unnecessary for the remainder of the earth roof commentary, but I will draw you a picture of the various roof layers for reference, which is Fig. 5.39. Please refer to the drawing as you follow the text.

5. Install the drainage layer, consisting of two inches (5.1 centimeters) of #2 crushed stone. This is stone about an inch (2.5 centimeters) in diameter.

6. Over the crushed stone, install two to three inches (5.1 to 7.6 centimeters) of loose hay or straw, which will eventually compress and decompose down into a natural filtration mat. It keeps the crushed stone drainage layer free of soil.

Fig. 5.39: Roofing detail for a free-
standing earth roof using moss
sods to retain the earth.

Key:

1. Above-grade wall.

2. Heavy wooden rafter.

3. 2" x 6" T&G planking.

4. Aluminum flashing as drip
   edge.

5. W.R. Grace Bituthene™ 4000 or
   equal membrane.

6. 4" to 5" rigid-foam insulation

7. 1" rigid foam or half-inch
   fibreboard to protect
   membrane.

8. 6-mil black polyethylene.

9. 2" of #2 crushed stone
   drainage layer.

10. Hay or straw filtration mat.

11. Moss or grass sods cut from
    sandy soil, retain the earth at
    the edges.

12. 7" to 8" topsoil, planted.

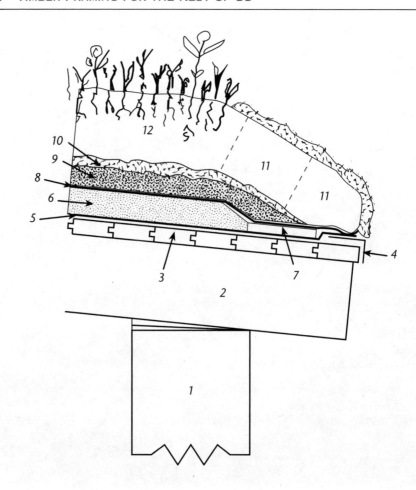

7. Over the hay or straw filtration mat, install enough earth to maintain a living roof. In temperate climates with moderate rainfall, eight inches (20.3 centimeters) is enough. Saturated earth weighs 120 pounds per cubic foot (1,922 kilos per cubic meter), so, to keep timber sizes down to something reasonable, we don't want to put any more earth up there than necessary.

8. Seed with whatever you like — grass, vetch, wildflowers. Mulch and water as necessary until the green cover is well established.

Closing In

With the timber framing completed, it was time to fill in the wall panels. We used the small lower panels beneath the windows as training panels for students at the building school, but, as we got higher, Jaki and I pandered to a dream which we have had for a long time: to make the most beautiful and artistic cordwood panels that we've ever done. The motif would be our Pacific Rim Journey of 2001, especially our one-week visit to Rapa Nui (Easter Island). The results of our efforts appear in the pictures at the end of this chapter. See my previous book, *Cordwood Building: The State of the Art* for more about cordwood masonry.

Windows and doors. I don't want to spend a lot of time on windows and doors. There are myriad choices. The most important consideration with respect to the subject matter of this book is that you may wish to frame the windows — and doors — with your heavy-timber posts and beams. This must be worked out carefully at the design stage. Know the rough opening (R.O.) of the windows and doors you plan to use, but don't trust figures in a catalog. There are such things as printer's errors, and Murphy's Law says that they will occur with the window that you intend to buy. Have the unit on site so that you can check the R.O.; then try it in place after you've done the framing.

We hired our friend John Light, a skilled builder, to help us install the five windows and our Therma-Tru™ exterior door. With John's help and experience, the job was done, and done right, in a day. I spent another day on the trim.

We have an exterior door in the sunroom, and an internal doorway connecting the new room with the dining room in the house. Both are framed to accommodate three-foot-wide (91-centimeter-wide) doors and both are located in 16-inch-wide cordwood walls, one 22 years old and one brand new. In each case, our doorframes consist of double-wide four-by-eight doorposts, with a similar lintel overhead. To join the two four-by-eights together into a single four-by-sixteen doorpost, I installed a vertical one-by-six "key," as seen in Fig. 5.40. Cordwood walls can be built right up to this key piece, and the log-ends can even touch it in the middle of the wall. Both the inner and outer mortar joints (each 5 inches wide) are laid up right against the doorpost, effectively locking the cordwood panel against the post. We use a similar detail at all post locations. Note also in Fig. 5.40 how a piece of angle iron is used to fasten the doorpost to the wooden deck. The angle iron, like the key piece, will wind up hidden in the cordwood wall.

The window on the west side is installed within a frame made from double-wide two-by-eight cedar planks, planed to 1⅞ inches (4.8 centimeters). The inner and outer components of the frame are scabbed together with a one-by-six (2.5-by-15.2 centimeter) key piece, similar to the one seen in Fig. 5.40. The frame "floats" in the cordwood wall, but is carefully centered. A strong lintel, seen in

Fig. 5.40: The one-by-six key piece locks the doorframe to the cordwood wall. The angle iron ties the doorpost to the floor.

Fig. 5.42 below, carries the load of the rafters down onto the cordwood wall.

Wood finishing. We sanded and varnished the window surrounds, and the posts and girders, but not the five-by-ten rafters. I used my trusty Makita 5"disk sander, #80 grit paper, to finish the timbers, some before construction, and some, as an afterthought, in situ. In retrospect, it would have been easier and more pleasant to do this sanding before installation. A belt sander is another option, but use a dust mask in either case. And listen to Mark Powers, one last time:

My new favorite tool is a Bosch portable 4" planer. It does a wonderful and relatively quick job of finishing the timbers before they're installed. My posts are sugar maple and the various beams are white ash, maple and beech. Once the grain is exposed, they are absolutely beautiful. I've used both a belt sander, and, now, the planer to finish timbers. Hands down, the planer is the way to go, yielding a beautiful almost glassy finish and removing only the bare minimum of wood. Besides revealing the natural beauty of the grain, finishing the timbers eliminates a lot of dust catching in the home.

We sanded the spruce floor and applied three coats of floor oil, which we had used successfully in the main part of the house. Something was different about the wood in the new room, though, and we found that shoes easily marked the oiled floor, and the marks were a real pain to clean. We finally broke down and, over the oil, applied two coats of Gym Seal, a hard clear surface used on gymnasium floors. Now the floor looks great and does not scuff.

The Finished Room

Following are some views (Figures 5.41–5.45) and details of the completed sunroom.

Jaki and I are glad that we have gained a beautiful new room as a result of this book … realizing that we wouldn't have built it otherwise! In case you're curious, the materials cost was about $4,000, or $20 per square foot. We also spent $250 on labor. And we also renewed the downstairs solar room at the same time, another 200 square feet, so we're quite pleased with the cost. Larger buildings could cost less per square foot, particularly as our sunroom is heavy on windows ($1,243 for five) and an exterior door ($338), expensive items. I believe that a timber-frame home, using techniques described in this book, combined with some sort of natural infilling (cob, cordwood, straw bale, wattle-and-daub, etc.) can still be built today for a materials cost of $15 to $25 per square foot, depending on where you build and how good you are at scrounging materials.

Now I hope that *Timber Framing for the Rest of Us* will inspire you to build with heavy timbers, joined by simple common-sense techniques and fasteners, and that your results will be every bit as satisfying as ours have been.

Just think, "build quality!"

Fig. 5.41a & b (detail, below): The completed sunroom at Earthwood. Only the cordwood snow-blocking in the lower solar room remains to be done. We also waited until the spring of 2003 to put the earth on the roof.

Fig. 5.42, near right: The west wall of the new sunroom. The double-wide four-by-eight lintel over the window carries the load down to the cordwood wall without placing pressure on the window itself.

Fig. 5.43, far right: The "Easter Island" panel at the new Earthwood sunroom. I wish you could see this in color, as the bottle-ends are beautiful.

Fig. 5.44, near right: Ceiling and rafter detail.

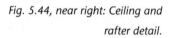

Fig. 5.45, far right: Joining two rafters with heavy metal plates can be quite attractive.

Appendix A: Span Tables

Using Span Tables

Table One is an abbreviated version of Table R502.3.1(2), from the International Residential Code for One- and Two- Family Dwellings. This particular table, just one of many in IRC codebook, is for floor joist spans for common lumber species, and assumes that we are designing for a residential living area with a live load of 40 pounds per square foot (40 PSF), a dead (structural) load of 10 PSF and an allowable deflection of 1/360.

Table Two is an abbreviated form of Table R802.5.1(7), from the International Residential Code for One- and Two- Family Dwellings. This table is helpful in designing rafter spans for anticipated 70 PSF snow loads on a 20 PSF dead load.

Let's do a couple of exercises, using Table Two:

Example 1: If I want rafters to be two-feet (24") on-center, what depth of rafter will I need to accommodate 12-foot spans?

Procedure: Go to the bottom — 24" — portion of the chart and look for spans of 12 feet and over. Only six of the strongest 2" × 10" will do it, the four select structural grades of all woods plus the Douglas fir-larch #1 and the Southern pine, #1. With 2" × 12" rafters — the last column — twelve of the sixteen listed woods will do the trick. Only the #3 grades — the weakest stuff — will not.

Example 2: I've scored a great deal on some 2" × 10" Southern pine #1 rafters. What is the greatest rafter span I can support?

Procedure: Go to the 2" × 10" column and look down until you spot Southern pine #1 for 16" and for 24"on-center spacings. At 16" centers, a span of 14' 4" is possible. At 24" centers, the span drops to 13' 1". These possible spans now need to be balanced against the size (length) of the desired building and the actual number of rafters "scored." The complete version of these span tables, as the appear in the International Building Code, also includes rafter spacings of 12" and 19.2" (0.5 meter).

Table 1: R502.3.1 (2) Floor Joist Spans for Common Lumber Species

Rafter Spacing (inches)	Species & Grade	2" × 6"	2" × 8"	2" × 10"	2" × 12"
	Allowable Deflection = 1/360		Dead Load = 10 psf		
			Maximum floor joist spans (feet & inches)		
16"	Douglas fir-larch SS	10'4"	13'7"	17'4"	21'1"
	Douglas fir-larch #1	9'11"	13'1"	16'5"	19'1"
	Douglas fir-larch #2	9'9"	12'7"	15'5"	17'10"
	Douglas fir-larch #3	7'6"	9'6"	11'8"	13'6"
	Hemlock-fir SS	9'9"	12'10"	16'5"	19'11"
	Hemlock-fir #1	9'6"	12'7"	16'0"	18'7"
	Hemlock-fir #2	9'1"	12'0"	15'"	17'7"
	Hemlock-fir #3	7'6"	9'6"	11'8"	13'6"
	Southern pine SS	10'2"	13'4"	17'0"	20'9"
	Southern pine #1	9'11"	13'1"	16'9"	20'4"
	Southern pine #2	9'9"	12'10"	16'1"	18'10"
	Southern pine # 3	8'1"	10'3"	12'2"	14'6"
	Spruce-pine-fir SS	9'6"	12'7"	16'0"	19'6"
	Spruce-pine-fir #1	9'4"	12'3"	15'5"	17'10"
	Spruce-pine-fir #2	9'4"	12'3"	15'5"	17'10"
	Spruce-pine-fir #3	7'6"	9'6"	11'8"	13'6"
24"	Douglas fir-larch SS	9'0"	11'11"	15'2"	18'5"
	Douglas fir-larch #1	8'8"	11'0"	13'5"	15'7"
	Douglas fir-larch #2	8'1"	10'3"	12'7"	14'7"
	Douglas fir-larch #3	6'2"	7'9"	9'6"	11'0"
	Hemlock-fir SS	8'6"	11'3"	14'4"	17'5"
	Hemlock-fir #1	8'4"	10'9"	13'1"	15'2"
	Hemlock-fir #2	7'11"	10'2"	12'5"	14'4"
	Hemlock-fir #3	6'2"	7'9"	9'6"	11'0"
	Southern pine SS	8'10"	11'8"	14'11"	18'1"
	Southern pine #1	8'8"	11'5"	14'7"	17'5"
	Southern pine #2	8'6"	11'0"	13'1"	15'5"
	Southern pine #3	6'7"	8'5"	9'11"	11'10"
	Spruce-pine-fir SS	8'4"	11'0"	14'0"	17'0"
	Spruce-pine-fir #1	8'1"	10'3"	12'7"	14'7"
	Spruce-pine-fir #2	8'1"	10'3"	12'7"	14'7"
	Spruce-pine-fir #3	6'2"	7'9"	9'6"	11'0"

Table 2: R802.5.1 (7) Rafter Spans for 70 PSF Ground Snow Load

Rafter Spacing (inches)	Species & Grade	2" × 4"	2" × 6"	2" × 8"	2" × 10"	2" × 12"
				Dead Load = 20 psf		
				(feet & inches)		
16"	Douglas fir-larch SS	6'10"	10'3"	13'0"	15'10"	18'4"
	Douglas fir-larch #1	5'10"	8'6"	10'9"	13'2"	15'3"
	Douglas fir-larch #2	5'5"	7'11"	10'1"	12'4"	14'3"
	Douglas fir-larch #3	4'1"	6'0"	7'7"	9'4"	10'9"
	Hemlock-fir SS	6'6"	10'1"	12'9"	15'7"	18'0"
	Hemlock-fir #1	5'8"	8'3"	10'6"	12'10"	14'10"
	Hemlock-fir #2	5'4"	7'10"	9'11"	12'1"	14'1"
	Hemlock-fir #3	4'1"	6'0"	7'7"	9'4"	10'9"
	Southern pine SS	6'9"	10'7"	14'0"	17'10"	21'0"
	Southern pine #1	6'5"	9'7"	12'0"	14'4"	17'1"
	Southern pine #2	5'10"	8'4"	10'9"	12'10"	15'1"
	Southern pine #3	4'4"	6'5"	8'3"	9'9"	11'7"
	Spruce-pine-fir SS	6'4"	9'6"	12'0"	14'8"	17'1"
	Spruce-pine-fir #1	5'5"	7'11"	10'1"	12'4"	14'3"
	Spruce-pine-fir #2	5'5"	7'11"	10'1"	12'4"	14'3"
	Spruce-pine-fir #3	4'1"	6'0"	7'7"	9'4"	10'9"
24"	Douglas fir-larch SS	6'5"	9'4"	11'10"	14'5"	16'9"
	Douglas fir-larch #1	5'4"	7'9"	9'10"	12'0"	13'11"
	Douglas fir-larch #2	5'0"	7'3"	9'2"	11'3"	13'0"
	Douglas fir-larch #3	3'9"	5'6"	6'11"	8'6"	9'10"
	Hemlock-fir SS	6'1"	9'2"	11'8"	14'2"	15'5"
	Hemlock-fir #1	5'2"	7'7"	9'7"	11'8"	13'7"
	Hemlock-fir #2	4'11"	7'2"	9'1"	11'1"	12'10"
	Hemlock-fir #3	3'9"	5'6"	6'11"	8'6"	9'10"
	Southern pine SS	6'4"	10'0"	13'2"	16'5"	19'2"
	Southern pine #1	5'11"	8'9"	11'0"	13'1"	15'7"
	Southern pine #2	5'4"	7'7"	9'10"	11'9"	13'9"
	Southern pine #3	4'0"	5'11"	7'6"	8'10"	10'7"
	Spruce-pine-fir SS	5'11"	8'8"	11'0"	13'5"	15'7"
	Spruce-pine-fir #1	5'0"	7'3"	9'2"	11'3"	13'0"
	Spruce-pine-fir #2	5'0"	7'3"	9'2"	11'3"	13'0"
	Spruce-pine-fir #3	3'9"	5'6"	6'11"	8'6"	9'10"

The tabulated rafter spans assume that ceiling joists are located at the bottom of the attic space or that some other method of resisting the outward push of the rafters on the bearing walls, such as rafter ties, is provided at that location.

Where to Find Span Tables

- **Books**. Seven of the books in the Bibliography have useful span tables, indicated by the notation (ST) before the entry. The International Residential Code for One- and Two-Family Dwellings has span tables that you know will be approved by code.

- **The Internet**. It is possible to find all sorts of span tables on the world wide web. I searched for span + tables on the popular Google search engine and came up with these excellent websites, among others:

www.southernpine.com/. This is the Southern Pine Council's website. Click on "Span Tables" for a list of over 40 different floor joist, ceiling joist, and roof rafter span tables using various grades of southern pine. Very comprehensive.

www.cwc.ca/design/design_tools/calcs/SpanCalc2002/index.php/. This is the Canadian Wood Councils Span Calc 2000 program. You can select the member type (rafter, floor joist, etc.), species of wood, grade, dimensions, spacing, and loads. Press "calculate" and the program instantly returns the maximum span. Despite being a Canadian website, the SpanCalc results are only valid in the United States.

www.wwpa.org/. This is the Western Wood Products comprehensive website. Click on "Span Tables Online," then "Individual Span Tables" and you will have access to dozens of span tables for rafters, floor joists, and ceiling joists. Various western wood species and grades are covered. You will need Acrobat Reader to download these.

Appendix B:
Stress Load Calculations for Beams

SPAN TABLES, LIKE THE ONE IN APPENDIX A, will serve for roof design with most structures. With heavy roofs, such as earth roofs, adequate tables are very hard to find. This Appendix shows how to check the girders and rafters in a heavy roof design for shear and bending. Once you have followed through the example, and understand where all the numbers have come from, you should be able to use the formulas and procedures to check other rectilinear designs. Two other books with good information about calculating beam strength are *A Timber Framer's Workshop* and *Homing Instinct*, both listed in Appendix C.

Using this Appendix requires familiarity with basic algebra, specifically the ability to substitute numbers for letters in a formula, and to solve for a single unknown. It is important to keep track of the units (feet, pounds, etc.) as you solve the equations. Please read Chapter 2: Basic Timber Frame Structure, before using this Appendix.

Problem: Test the 40- by 40-foot Log End Cave Plan for the shear and bending strength of the rafters and girders as designed. (The posts and planks are the strong — in some ways overbuilt — components of this design, as discussed in Chapter 2.) A portion of the plan, enough for our purposes, is shown in Fig. A2.1. Girders are labeled "beams" on the plan. The plan is based upon simple 10-foot-square sections, repeated sixteen times, like a chessboard with just four squares on a side. Only six complete sections are shown in the portion reproduced here. Here are the givens:

Design Load:

Earth roof, saturated; 8 inches at 10 pounds/inch/SF.....................80 pounds/SF

Crushed stone drainage layer; 2 inches at 10 pounds/inch/SF ....20 pounds/SF

Snow load by code, Plattsburgh, NY..70 pounds/SF

Structural load, typical for scale of heavy timber structure

(includes timbers, planking, membrane, and insulation) ....15 pounds/SF

Total maximum load ....185 pounds/SF

Kind and grade of wood:

Different species of woods have different stress load ratings, and the lumber grade has a large impact on the ratings, too, as can be seen from these few examples from *Architectural Graphic Standards*:

Type of wood	Grade	f_b[1]	f_v[2]
Douglas Fir, Inland Region	Select Structural	2,150	145
Douglas Fir, Inland Region	Common Structural	1,450	95
Eastern Hemlock	Select Structural	1,300	85
Eastern Hemlock	Common Structural	1,100	60
Southern Pine	#1 Dense	1,700	150
Southern Pine	#2	1,100	85

[1] unit stress for bending in pounds per square inch
[2] unit stress for shear in pounds per square inch

For our example, all timbers are assumed to be Douglas Fir (Inland Region, Common Structural) with the following stress load values:

Unit stress for bending (fb) of 1,450 pounds per square inch
Unit stress for horizontal shear (fv) of 95 pounds per square inch

These are moderate values, incidentally, similar to Eastern spruce and red and white pine. See *Architectural Graphic Standards*, *The Encyclopedia of Wood*, *A Timber Framers Workshop* and other engineering manuals for stress load ratings for a variety of woods.

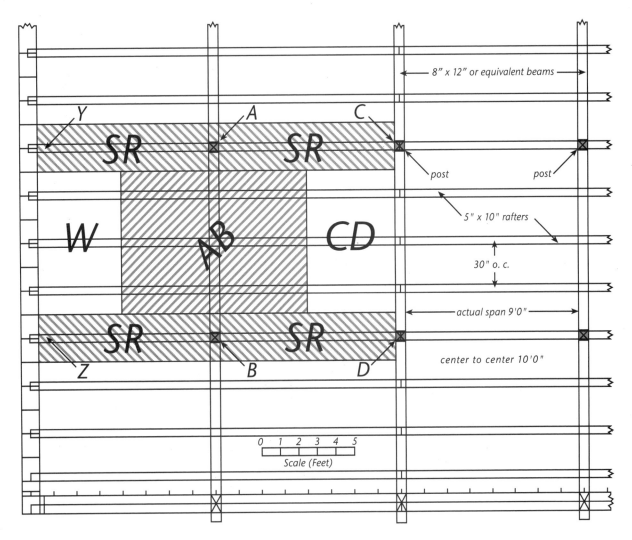

Fig. A2.1: A portion of the 40' x 40' Log End Cave plan.

Cross-sectional dimensions (b and d):

- Rafters are "five-by-tens," that is, they are five inches (12.7 cm) in breadth (b) and ten inches (25.4 cm) in depth (d).
- Girders ("beams" on the plan) are "eight-by-twelves," that is, they are eight inches (20.3 cm) in breadth (b) and twelve inches (30.5 cm) in depth (d).

Frequency (spacing):

- Rafters are 30 inches o.c., that is: 30 inches (76 cm) is the center-to-center spacing for adjacent members.

- Girders are 10 feet o.c., that is: ten feet (3 m) is the center-to-center spacing between parallel girders or between girders and the side walls.

Span (L):

- Spans are nominally ten feet (3 m) for both girders and rafters. Actual clear spans, from the edge of one support to the edge of another, is closer to nine feet (2.75 m), but 10 feet is the number used in place of L (span) in the example.

Nomenclature:

- "Beam" refers to both rafters and girders
- "Simple Span" means that a beam is supported only at its ends. For example, the top half of Fig. 2.10 on page 24 shows two simple-span beams.
- "Double Span" means that a beam is supported at its ends, and also at its midpoint, as in the bottom half of Fig. 2.10.

A = Cross-sectional area (b times d) of beam in square inches

b = Breadth of beam, in inches

d = Depth of beam, in inches

f_b = Allowable unit stress for bending in pounds per square inch

f_v = Allowable unit stress for shear in pounds per square inch

L = Length of span in feet

M = Bending moment in foot-pounds or inch-pounds

M_x = Bending moment at the two midspans on a double-span beam

PSF = pounds per square foot

R = Reaction at supports

S = Section modulus of cross-section of beam in inches cubed

V = Total shear allowable or actual

w = Load or weight per linear foot on beam, in pounds

W = Total uniform load or weight on beam, in pounds

Algebraic operations:

$/$ = The division sign. The value before the division sign is divided by the value after it.

6(8) = 48 or (6)(8) = 48 means "6 times 8 equals 48." The "times" sign is implied.

bd = A means "b times d equals A." Again, multiplication is implied.

Formulas used with Simple-Spans:

$R = V = wL/2$ $M = wL/8$ $S = bd^2/6$

$S = M/f_b$ $f_v = 3V/2A$ $V = wL/2$

Formulas used with Double Spans:

$R_1 = V_1 = R_3 = V_3 = 3wL/8$ $R_2 = 2V_2 = 10wL/8$

$V_2 = 5wL/8$ $M_x = 9wL^2/128$

We have now listed the five variables for structural design for shear and bending, as discussed in Chapter 2, and we have all the nomenclature and formulas that we need. Now we want to find out if the structure as designed — particularly the rafters and girders — is of adequate strength for both shear and bending to support the design load of 185 pounds per square foot (903 kilos per square meter).

1. Calculating roof load for bending for rafters, simple-span.

(That is, all rafters are about ten feet long, and join over girders.)

$S = bd^2/6 = (5")(10")^2/6 = 83.3$ in^3 (Section modulus is measured in "inches cubed")

$f_b = 1,450$ psi (pounds/square inch), given above for Douglas Fir, Inland Region, Common Structural

$S = M/f_b$. By transposition: $M = S(f_b) = 83.3$in^3 (1450 lb/in^2) = 120,785 in. lbs

This is the bending moment in "inch-pounds". To derive the more convenient "foot-pounds," we need to divide by 12 in/ft, because there are 12 inches in a foot. So:

120,785 in. lbs divided by 12 in/ft = 10,065 foot-pounds

L = 10' (given). $M = wL^2/8$.   By transposition: $w = 8M/L^2$

Substituting for M and L: $w = 8(10,065$ ft lbs$)/100$ ft^2 = 805 lbs/ft

That is: 805 pounds per linear foot. We haven't got pounds per square feet quite yet. If rafters were on 12-inch centers, they could support 805 pounds per square foot (3,930 kilos per square meter). A linear foot would translate to a square foot in this special case. But our example calls for rafters on 30-inch centers, so we need to make the following adjustment:

12"/sq. ft. divided by 30" = 0.4 ft.(805 lbs/ft) = 322 **PSF** allowable

Think of it this way: There are only 40 percent (0.4) as many rafters on 30-inch centers as on 12-inch centers. As the impact of frequency is a direct proportional relationship to strength, the rafters on 30-inch centers will support only 40 percent of the load, everything else remaining the same.

The specified rafters, on simple span, will easily support the 185 PSF required.

Now lets try it on a double span. We'll use 20-foot-long rafters, supported at each end, but also at the middle by a girder.

2. **Calculating roof load for bending for rafters, double-span. (That is, all rafters are about twenty feet long, and supported at midspan by a girder.)**

Maximum allowable bending moment (M) = 10,065 foot pounds, from calculation (1) above.

M_x = Bending moment at the two midspans on a double-span beam

$M_x = 9wL^2/128$ (from formulas above)

$W = 128\,M_x/9L^2$ $w = 128(10{,}065\ \text{ft. lbs.})/9(10\ \text{ft})^2 = 1431\ \text{lbs./ft}$

Again, this is "pounds per linear foot." We make the same adjustment that we made at the end of calculation (1) above:

12"/sq. ft divided by 30" = 0.4 ft.(1,431 lbs/ft) = 572 **PSF** allowable

Using a single 20-footer, supported halfway, increases bending strength by quite a bit, but this value is far stronger than it needs to be. Now, lets test rafters for shear.

3. Calculating roof load for shear on simple-span.

f_v = 95 psi (pounds/square inch), given above for the same grade of Douglas Fir

A = bd = 5"(10") = 50 inches squared (In this case, the same as "square inches.")

f_v = 3V/2A. By transposition: V = 2Af_v/3 = 2(50 in²)(95 lbs)/3(in²) = 3,167 pounds maximum allowable (V is "total shear allowable")

V = wL/2. So, w = 2V/L = 2(3,167 lbs)/10 feet = 633 pounds per (linear) foot

But, again, rafters are not on 12" centers, but are actually 30 inches o.c. Making the adjustment: 12"/30" = 0.4 0.4(633) = 253 **PSF** allowable, another good strong number.

4. Calculating roof load for shear on a double-span rafter.

Maximum allowable shear (V) = 3,167 pounds from calculation (3) above.

Shear at ends (R_1 and R_3): V = 3wL/8. Transposed: w = 8V/3L

W = 8(3,167 pounds)/3(10 feet) = 845 pounds per lineal foot

Rafters are 30 inches o.c., so: 12"/30" = 0.4; 0.4(845) = 338 pounds per square foot

That is the shear strength at the ends, at R_1 and R_3. But, at R_2, the center support, the situation is a little different:

Shear at middle (R_2): V = 5wL/8. Transposed: w = 8V/5L

W = 8(3,167 pounds)/5(10 feet) = 507 pounds per lineal foot

Rafters are 30 inches o.c., so: 12"/30" = 0.4; 0.4(507) = 203 **PSF**, still more than the 185 PSF foot required.

Now let's do the girders, and we'll just do them for single-span because 20-foot-plus eight-by-twelve girders are really a bit extreme. Plus, as we know, they will not only be easier to install as two 10-footers, but the shorter pieces will actually be stronger on shear.

5. **Calculating roof load for bending on the single span 8- by 12-inch Douglas fir girders of this example. The load from the rafters is symmetrically placed along the girder at regular 30-inch spacings, so it is reasonable to use the same formulas we used for single-span rafters.**

$S = bd^2/6 = (8")(12")^2/6 = 192 \ in^3$ (Section modulus is measured in "inches cubed")

$f_b = 1450$ psi (pounds/square inch), given above for Douglas Fir, Inland Region, Common Structural

$S = M/f_b$. By transposition: $M = S(f_b)$ $M = 192 in^3 (1,450 \ lb/in^2) = 278,400$ in. lbs

This is the bending moment in "inch pounds". To derive the more convenient "foot pounds," we need to divide by 12 in/ft, because there are 12 inches in a foot. So:

278,400 in. lbs divided by 12 in/ft = 23,200 foot pounds

$L = 10'$ (given) $M = wL^2/8$. By transposition: $w = 8M/L^2$

Substituting for M and L: $w = 8(23,200 \ ft \ lbs)/100 \ ft^2 = 1,856$ pounds per linear foot

The girder can support 1,856 pounds per linear foot, or 18,560 pounds in all, if the load is fairly constant along its length. But for what portion of the roof is the girder responsible? Look again at Fig. A2.1. The area AB is the area for which girder A-B is responsible. Area CD is part of the area carried by the girder C-D. Area W is carried by the block wall. The two areas labeled SR are carried by the special rafters labeled Y and Z. Y and Z are special because their loads are carried directly down through the girders to the posts, adding no bending stresses to the girder. The area AB is 10 feet by 7.5 feet or 75 square feet. So, the total allowable carrying capacity of the girder (18,560 pounds in all) divided by the square footage for which it is responsible (75 square feet) results in the allowable load per square foot, assuming an equally distributed load. 18,560 pounds/75 SF = 247.5 **PSF**. Still a good number, as it is higher than 185 PSF. Now, what about girders on shear?

6. **Calculating roof load for shear on the single span 8" by 12" Douglas fir girders of this example. The load from the rafters is symmetrically placed along the girder at regular 30-inch spacings, so it is reasonable to use the same formulas we used for single-span rafters.**

f_v = 95 psi (pounds/square inch), given above for the same grade of Douglas Fir

A = bd = 6"(12") = 96 inches squared (In this case, the same as "square inches.")

$f_v = 3V/2A$. By transposition: $V = 2Af_v/3 = 2(96 \text{ in}^2)(95 \text{ lbs})/3(\text{in}^2) = 6{,}080$ pounds maximum allowable (V is "total shear allowable")

To get the shear strength at the ends of a single-span rafter, use:

$V = wL/2$ So, $w = 2V/L = 2(6{,}080 \text{ lbs})/10 \text{ feet} = 1{,}216$ pounds per (linear) foot, or 12,160 pounds over 10 feet.

Again, the area for which girder A-B is responsible is area AB, or 75 SF.

12,160 pounds divided by 75 SF results in 162.1 **PSF**, which is less than the desired carrying capacity of 185 PSF for the earth roof described. It doesn't look good. However, if we consider that the true girder clear span (between posts) is actually 9 foot 4 inches and substitute 9 foot 4 inches (9.333') for 10 feet in w = 2V/L, we get w = 1,303 pounds per linear foot, or 13,030 over 10 feet. Divided by 75 SF results in 173.7 **PSF**, closer, but still a little short of the mark. What can we do? Shear, unlike bending, is a direct linear relationship. The shortfall can be made up in variety of ways. These will all work:

A. Beef the girders up to 9 inches wide. Now A = 108 square inches instead of 96 square inches. This change increases the cross-sectional area of the girder — and its shear strength — by 12.5 percent because 12/96 = .125. Now, 173.7 PSF times 1.125 equals 195.4 **PSF**, so we're good again.

B. Use a wood with a unit stress for horizontal shear at least 10 percent greater than the 95 psi for Douglas Fir (Inland Region, Common Structural). Any wood with an (f_v) of at least 105 psi would do nicely.

C. Shorten the girder clear span by 7 inches to 8 foot 9 inches (8.75'). This yields 185.3 **PSF**, which is fine, as there are great safety factors built into these calculations. Just work to the numbers. You don't have to add an additional safety factor.

D. If you want to keep the plan as designed, you could always decrease the load by about 12 PSF, down to 173 PSF. Eliminate 1.2 inches of earth or crushed stone. Is this cheating? In point of fact, the stone and earth layers at Earthwood are really about 8.5 inches total, not 10 inches, so our load here is probably about 170 PSF. This is enough to maintain our living roof.

Incidentally, using a 20-foot girder, supported half way, weakens the plan unacceptably in terms of shear strength for the girders. While shear strength increases at the ends to 218 PSF, it decreases over the center support to 130 PSF. Strange, but true. See Fig. 2.10 and the nearby commentary in Chapter 2 under the heading Shear and Shear Failure.

Disclaimer: The author is not an engineer. Use these exercises as a point of beginning, to get you into the ballpark. Always have your plan checked by a qualified structural engineer.

Appendix C: Resources

Building Schools

Traditional Timber Framing

Black Rapids Timber Framing School
1307 Windfall Way, Fairbanks, AK 99709
Telephone: (907) 455•6158
Website: www.blackrapids.org
New kids on the block. Check their website.

Fox Maple School of Traditional Building
P.O. Box 249, Brownfield, ME 04010
Telephone: (207) 935•3720
Website: www.foxmaple.com
Teaches courses in traditional timber framing, both at their Maine campus, and even in exotic places such as Costa Rica and Kauai, Hawaii.

Heartwood School
Johnson Hill Road, Washington, MA 01223
Telephone: (413) 623•6677
Website: www.heartwoodschool.com
Conducts a variety of house-building courses, but specializes in traditional timber framing through their affiliation with the Timber Framer's Guild.

Murray Timber & Panel Systems LLC
4262 NE 125 Street, Seattle, WA 98125
Telephone: (206) 417•2212

Website: www.murraytimber.com
Conducts weekend and week-long workshops in timber framing from May to
October, in Carnation, Washington and Grants Pass, Oregon.

North House Folk School
P.O. Box 759, Grand Marais, MN 55604
Telephone: (218) 387•9762
Website: www.northhousefolkschool.com
Classes in timber framing.

Yestermorrow Design/Build School
189 VT Route 100, Warren, VT 05674
Telephone: (802) 496•5545 or (888) 496•5541
Website: www.yestermorrow.org
Teaches a variety of design-build courses, including traditional timber framing.

Other

Earthwood Building School
366 Murtagh Hill Road, West Chazy, NY 12992
Telephone: (518) 493•7744
Website: www.cordwoodmasonry.com
Conducts workshops in cordwood masonry and earth-sheltered housing, in
northern New York, and around the world. Cordwood masonry makes excellent
infilling within a post-and-beam frame. Earthwood will begin conducting 3-day
"Timber Framing for the Rest of Us" workshops in 2004, using this book as a
text. Several buildings at Earthwood are made using these techniques.

Cob Cottage Company
Box 123, Cottage Grove, OR 97425
Telephone: (541) 942•2005
Website: www.cobcottage.com
Teaches cob construction and other natural building methods in Oregon,
Mexico, and other locations. Cob is an excellent infilling option for timber
framing in warm to moderate climates.

Organizations

Structural Insulated Panels (SIPs)

Structural Insulated Panel Association
P.O. Box 1699, Gig Harbor, WA 98335
Telephone: (253) 858•7472
Website: www.sips.org
The Internet site is useful. Click on "Find Panels" for a comprehensive list of companies that manufacture stress-skin panels. These insulated panels have become the method of choice for skinning a timber-frame home. All sorts of siding can be installed over them. The timber frame is left exposed on the interior.

Timber Framing

Timber Frame Business Council
17 Main Street, Hamilton, MT 59840
Telephone: (406) 375•0713 or (888) 560•9251
Website: www.timberframe.org
This not-for-profit organization is "dedicated to increasing awareness of the benefits of timber-frame construction." You can get a list of timber frame companies — and magazines — at their website.

Timber Framers Guild
P.O. Box 60, Becket, MA 01223
Telephone: (888) 453•0879
Website: www.tfguild.org
Publishes *Scantlings*, a timber-frame newsletter and *Timber Framing*, a small but informative and well-produced quarterly magazine. Subscriptions are $25 per year. Workshops conducted in association with Heartwood (see Building Schools).

Grading of Lumber

Northeastern Lumber Manufacturers Association (NeLMA)
P.O. Box 87A, Cumberland, ME 04021
Telephone: (207) 829•6901
Website: www.nelma.org
Get structural values here for eastern softwoods, including hemlock, spruce, and white pine. NeLMA has several softwood grading inspectors on their staff.

National Hardwood Association
6830 Raleigh LaGrange Road, Memphis, TN 38184
Telephone: (901) 377•1818
Website: www.natlhardwood.org
All about grading of hardwoods, including a list of hardwood graders in North America.

Manufacturers

Fasteners

Cleveland Steel Specialty Company
26001 Richmond Road, Bedford Heights, OH 44146
Telephone: (216) 464•9400
Website: www.ClevelandSteel.com
Makers of a variety of wood-to-wood and wood-to-concrete connectors.

GRK Canada, Ltd.
1499 Rosslyn Road, Thunder Bay, ON P7E 6W1 Canada
Telephone: (800) 263•0463
Website: www.grkfasteners.com
Distributors of GRK Fasteners, including extremely strong and tough long screws for joining heavy timbers.

Olympic Manufacturing Group, Inc.

153 Bowles Road, Agawam, MA 01001

Website: www.olyfast.com

Telephone: 1 (800) 633•3800

Manufacturers of TimberLok™ screws for joining heavy timbers, described in Chapter 4.

Simpson Strong-Tie Company, Inc.

4120 Dublin Boulevard, Suite 400, Dublin, CA 94568

Telephone: (925) 560•9000 or (800) 999•5099

Website: www.strongtie.com

Makers of a full line of wood-construction connectors and fasteners for tying wooden members down to foundations.

Timberlinx, Division of Michael Preston Distributors Ltd.

5 Jean Dempsey Gate, West Hill, ON M1C 3C1, Canada

Telephone: (416) 284•8934

Website: www.timberlinx.com

Suppliers of strong bolt-type connectors, used in place of mortise and tenon – and other – timber framing joints.

USP Lumber Connectors

703 Rogers Drive, Montgomery, MN 56069-1324

Telephone: (800) 328•5934

Website: www.USPconnectors.com

Makes a full line of lumber connectors.

Tools

Bailey's

196 Edwards Drive, Jackson, TN 38301

Telephone: (731) 422•1300 or (800) 322•4539

Website: www.baileys-online.com

Family-run mail order company with a great selection of chainsaws, logging safety equipment, chainsaw mills, and portable sawmills.

Beam Machine, Ted Mather
Box 16, Quathiaski Cove, BC V0P 1N0, Canada
Telephone: (250) 384•9210 or US only: (800) 609•2160
Website: www.beammachine.com
Ted Mather makes and supplies the inexpensive Beam Machine chainsaw attachment.

Granberg International – Alaska Chainsaw Mill
P.O. Box 2347, Vallejo, CA 94592
Telephone: (866) 233•6499
Website: www.granberg.com
Makes the Granberg Mini-Mill, Small Log Mill, and the various Alaskan MK-III mills for chainsaws.

Haddon Tools – Haddon Lumbermaker
21967 West Vernon Ridge Drive, Mundelein, IL 60060
Telephone: (888) 705•1911
Website: www.haddontools.com
Haddon makes the Haddon Lumbermaker, which performed well as a low-cost chainsaw mill during tests conducted at Earthwood Building School.

***Independent Sawmill and Woodlot Management Magazine*, Sawmill Publishing**
31 Central Street, Suite 214, Bangor, ME 04401
Telephone: (888) 290•9469
Website: www.sawmillmag.com
This magazine has articles about small personal sawmills, woodlot management, seasoning lumber, and related subjects. Some articles are available on their website. They review small sawmill attachments frequently and manufacturers advertise in their pages.

Logolsol, Inc.
P.O. Box 660, Madison, MS 39130
Telephone: (877) 564•6765
Makes the Logosol Timber Jig.

Muskegon Power Tool

2357 Whitehall Road, Muskegon, MI 49445

Telephone: (800) 635•5465

Makers of the Linear Link® chainsaw adaptor for a circular saw. Works as a beam cutter.

Prazi Beam Cutter

118 Long Pond Road, Plymouth, MA 02360

Telephone: (800) 262•0211

Another manufacturer of a chainsaw-type beam cutter adaptor kit for a circular saw.

SIR Incorporated – Better Built Ripsaw

P.O. Box 266, 5700 Columbus City Road, Grant, AL 35747

Telephone: (256) 728•3070

Website: www.sirscottsboro.com

SIR, which stands for Southeastern Industrial Resources, is now the manufacturer of the Better Built Ripsaw described on page 57.

Structural Insulated Panels

Winter Panel Corporation

74 Glen Orne Drive, Brattleboro, VT 05301

Telephone: (802) 254•3435

Website: www.winterpanel.com

This company does a lot of work with timber framers, but is only one of dozens of such manufacturers. They have an excellent explanatory website about SIPs. Go to the Structural Insulated Panel Association's website (see Organizations, above) for a thorough list of manufacturers.

Glossary of Terms

A

Alaskan slab: See slab on grade

Adz: A heavy chisel-like steel tool mounted at right angles to a wooden handle. Used for hewing square timbers from a tree trunk.

Angle clips: Strong, economical right-angle connectors for fastening a vertical member to a horizontal member.

B

Balloon framing: A modern conventional frame of two-by construction in which vertical members (studs) run all the way to the top-story plate.

Beam: Generally, a heavy timber laid horizontally. Rafters, joists, and girders are all different kinds of beams.

Bent: A section of timber framing fastened together on the ground or floor and raised in one piece.

Board foot: The measure by which lumber is sold. A board foot (BF) is one inch (2.5 centimeters) thick by one foot (30.5 centimeters) wide by one foot (30.5 centimeters) long, or 144 cubic inches (2,360 cubic centimeters) of wood.

Bending strength: The ability of a beam to resist failure under a load, along its length. Bending failure generally occurs by a snapping of the timber somewhere in the middle third of its length.

Bird's Mouth: A triangular notch cut into a rafter so that the vertical load bears straight down on the girt, so-called because of a resemblance to a bird's open beak.

Brace: A temporary support for a post or a bent, usually a scrap board fastened diagonally to the member to be braced and well-staked to the ground, or fastened to the floor. Also called "wind braces."

C

Cantilever: A horizontal projection of a beam over a supporting wall.

Carriage bolt: A bolt with one end threaded to receive a nut, and the other end rounded with a square countersink below the head. As the bolt is tightened, the square part of the shaft is drawn into the wood. Because of the rounded head, the wood surface is left fairly smooth on one side.

Centroid: The neutral center line running longitudinally along the length of a horizontal beam, also called the neutral axis.

Chord: In a truss, the top or bottom timbers.

Column: A post or pillar

Column base: A mechanical fastener for tying a column or post to a concrete foundation. Also called a "post base."

Compression: A force that presses or squeezes. Blocks in a stack are "in compression."

Combined load: The sum total of all of the loads which act on a frame, also called the "resultant load."

Conventional frame: Plywood-and-stud construction. See stud.

Cross cut: To saw perpendicular to the grain of the wood.

D

Dead load: The combined load of all the materials that make up a structure, sometimes called the "structural load."

Deflection: A bending downward.

Dovetail joint: A joint formed by a number of mortise and tenons spread in the shape of a dove's tail. Common joint in furniture making for joining two boards at a corner.

E

Eaves: The overhanging lower edge of a roof.

Expansion shield, Expansion anchor: Mechanical devices used for fastening plates or pins into concrete.

F

Floating slab: See slab-on-grade.

Frequency: The spacing of rafters or joists: 12 inches on center, 16 inches o.c., 24 inches o.c., etc.

G

Gable, Gable End: The end-wall face of a ridged roof, usually triangular.

Girder: A large timber or beam which carries floor joists, often called a "summer beam" by traditional timber framers.

Girt: Horizontal timbers that join the tops of posts around the perimeter of a timber-framed building. Sidewall girts often support floor joists in some way.

Grading: A determination of a wood's quality for structural or other purposes, normally done by a professional wood grader.

H

Hanger: In timber framing for the rest of us, any metal fastener used to hang a joist or rafter on a girt, girder, or foundation wall.

J

Joint: The intersection of two timbers.

Joist: Horizontal members which support decks, floors, ceilings, etc. If supporting the roof, these members are known as rafters.

K

Kerf: The cut produced by a saw, or the wood lost by making a cut.

L

Lag bolt: A hex-headed bolt with a thread that will accept a hex-shaped nut. Used for drawing two pieces of wood together.

Lag screw: A heavy screw with a hex head, turned directly into wood (or into expansion shields.). Will not accept a nut. Useful for fastening heavy metal plates to beams.

Lintel: A horizontal member bridging a door, window or other opening.

Load: The total force acting upon a structure.

Live load: The anticipated load over and above the structure's own weight, such as furniture, people, snow, earth, etc.

M

Metal plate: A piece of heavy metal used to join two or more adjacent timbers. The plates can be useful in a variety of shapes: rectangular, T-shaped, L-shaped, etc.

Mortise: The cavity that accepts the tenon in a mortise-and- tenon joint.

Mortise-and-tenon joint: One of the more common joints in traditional timber framing, used to join one timber to the side of another. A carved tenon — the male member — is inserted into a mortise, the female member. Wooden pegs make the joint fast.

N

Neutral axis: See centroid.

O

On center (o.c.): The spacing of horizontal joists or rafters. The distance from the center of one member to the center of the next, usually in inches, as 16 inches o.c..

Overhang: The projection of the roof beyond the wall that supports it.

P

Pad: In foundation parlance, a substrate built up of a good percolating material such as coarse sand, gravel, or crushed stone.

Pegs, Pins: Wooden dowels used to make joints fast in traditional timber framing.

Pitch: See roof pitch.

Plate: On a foundation, the transitional wooden piece between concrete and the timber frame, often pressure treated. In this usage, sill or sill plate is the same. The term is also used by timber framers as the name of the longitudinal piece which joins a number of transverse bents together. See also metal plate.

Platform frame: See stick frame.

Plumb: Conforming to a true vertical line. Can be checked with a plumb bob or the vertical bubble of a carpenter's level.

Plumb bob: A weight on a string used to check vertical trueness.

Post: The main vertical member in timber-frame construction. Also column.

Post and beam: A structural system in which loads are carried by heavy vertical timbers (posts) and horizontal members (beams). May be fastened with hardware or by traditional timber framing joinery.

Purlin: A secondary roof timber spanning between primary rafters, usually horizontally.

R

Rabbet: A rectangular recess made along the edge of a timber, made to receive a similarly shaped piece. "Rabbet joints" usually form a right-angled corner.

Rafter: The timbers spanning from the eaves of the house to its ridge. Roof sheathing is attached to the rafters, although horizontal purlins sometimes intervene.

Reinforcing bar, Rebar: A length of ribbed steel used to provide tensile strength to concrete. Generally available in 10- and 20-foot lengths, and a variety of diameters.

Ridge: The horizontal apex of a roof.

Ridgepole, Ridge beam: A horizontal timber that follows the ridge or apex of a roof.

Rip: To saw wood parallel to the grain. A chainsaw mill rips the log into timbers.

Roof pitch: The ratio of roof rise to the span of the building, expressed as a fraction, such as ¼ or ⅓ pitch.

Roof slope: A ratio of the height of the ridge to the half-span of the building. Also a ratio of the roof rise to its run. For example, a three-in-twelve slope (expressed 3:12) indicates that the slope rises 3 feet vertically for every 12 feet of horizontal run.

S

Scarf: To join two beams to make a longer one. There are a variety of time-tested scarf joints used in traditional timber framing, but mechanical fasteners can also be used.

Shake: The separation of layers of wood along the annual growth rings.

Sill: In traditional timber framing, the timber that ties the bottom of a sidewall or gable end bent together, also called a "groundsill." With modern conventional building, the sill is the plate that runs along the top of the foundation wall. See also plate.

Shear strength: The ability of a horizontal beam to resist shear failure under a load. Shear failure generally occurs in a beam right over a supporting post or girder, where opposing tension and compression forces cause a rupture of the wood.

Slab: With foundations, a flat concrete floor or foundation base. At the sawmill, the first piece cut from a log being milled.

Slab on grade: A foundation system in which a slab is supported by a pad of percolating material. Used as an alternative means of frost protection, as opposed to sinking footings down below anticipated maximum frost levels.

Slenderness ratio (S.R.): A ratio of a post's length to its narrowest width. The lower the number, the stronger the post.

Slope: See roof slope.

Span: The clear distance between one support and another, as in "The girder has a ten-foot span."

Stick frame: Modern conventional wall framing using studs and other "two-by" lumber, such as two-by-fours and two-by-sixes.

Stress skin panel: See structural insulated panel.

Strike bolt: A threaded bolt installed into a hole in a concrete substrate by striking an expansion pin with a hammer.

Structural insulated panel (SIP): A manufactured panel, with sandwiched layers which include an outer sheathing, insulation, vapor barrier and internal sheathing. Regularly sized, SIPS have become a common method of wall-building applied to the exterior of traditional timber frames.

Stud: In conventional – or "stick-built" – framing, the vertical members, generally made from two-by-fours or two-by-sixes.

Summer: In traditional timber framing, a major horizontal timber which spans the girts. Can also serve the purpose of a tie beam.

T

Tenon: A cut or carved projection at the end of a wooden framing member which fits into a mortise to make a joint.

Tension: Stretching force. A string supporting a stone is "in tension."

Tie beam: A transverse timber which ties the two sidewalls together, keeping them parallel and preventing outward spread.

Tie-downs: A metal strap or fastener used to tie one structural system to another, as wall to foundation, or roof system to wall.

Tie plates: Flat metal plates, drilled with a series of holes, used to join one beam to another.

Timber: All-inclusive term referring to a post, beam, girder, rafter, girt, summer, etc. Also, standing wood in a forest, as "a stand of timber."

Timber frame: A structural framework made from timbers. "Traditional timber framing" makes use of wooden pegs and time-honored wood-to-wood jointing methods. "Timber framing for the rest of us" makes use of nails, screws, bolts, metal plates, and other mechanical fasteners to join wood together in a strong way.

TimberLok™ screws: Trade name for special screws made for joining heavy timbers, manufactured by Olympic Manufacturing Group, listed in Appendix C.

Toe nail, Toe screw: To fasten a vertical member to a horizontal one by driving nails (or screws) from one member to the other on about a 60-degree angle.

Top plate: In conventional stick-frame construction, the horizontal timber along the top of a framed wall. Also called "roof plate." With timber framing, the top plate can mean the same thing, but girt is also correct.

Tongue-in-groove, Tongue-and-groove: A floor- or roof-decking system whereby adjacent boards are strengthened by the tongue (milled projection) of one plank being inserted into a milled "groove" on its fellow. Abbreviated T & G or T-in-G, etc.

Truss: A rigid unit of timbers with pre-engineered tension and compression members, often triangular, which can carry roof loads over the transverse span of a building.

Truss plates: Tie plates used in the manufacture of trusses. Some have hundreds of little spikes sticking out of them and are applied under pressure by special machinery.

V

Viga: A rafter or joist with a round cross-section, common in Southwestern and Mexican architecture.

W

Wane: The rounded edge of a post or beam resulting from the timber being cut from a slightly undersized log.

Western frame: See stick frame.

Bibliography

I USED MOST OF THESE BOOKS TO RESEARCH *Timber Framing For the Rest of Us*. A few have been added because they cover related subjects that may be of interest, such as works on various kinds of infilling methods. The notation (ST) before the entry indicates a book containing useful span tables.

Structure

(ST) Ambrose, James and Harry Parker. *Simplified Design of Wood Structures*. John Wiley and Sons, 1994. ISBN: 0-471-17989-2; 0-471-30366-6. *Expensive ($80) but comprehensive, this book is a practical introduction to the design of wood structures. It is written for those with limited experience in engineering or advanced mathematics, with sections on structural properties, stress load calculations, lumber gradings, and use classification. You can sometimes get a good used copy at www.amazon.com for about $45, as I did, but try the library first.*

Ching, Francis D.K. *Building Construction Illustrated*, Third Edition. John Wiley & Sons, 2001. ISBN: 0-471-35898-3. *This is the poor man's Architectural Graphic Standards. Ching's drawing shows just about everything there is in normal building construction, from foundation to roof.*

Forest Products Laboratory. *The Encyclopedia of Wood*. Sterling, 1980. ISBN: 0-8069-8890-8. *Contains the mechanical (and other) properties of almost every wood you can think of. It is too bad that this book is out of print, but a lot of copies were printed, so look for it*

in used bookstores and at the library. (This is good advice for all the books listed here.)

Gordon, J.E. *Structures: or Why Things Don't Fall Down*. Da Capo Press, 1978. ISBN: 0-306-80151-5. *Back in the 1980s, this one gave me my first inkling of how structures actually work. A classic. Highly entertaining, therefore educational.*

Hoadley, R. Bruce. *Identifying Wood*. Taunton Press, 1990. ISBN: 0-942391-04-7. *Before you can do any reasonable structural analysis, you have to know what kind of wood you've got. This comprehensive book will take you through the genus level of wood identification.*

Hoadley, R. Bruce. *Understanding Wood*. Taunton Press. 2000. ISBN: 1-56158-358-8. *All about wood's properties, including its nature, structure, shrinking, and swelling. Wood identification is covered, but not as comprehensively as in Hoadley's Identifying Wood.*

(ST) International Code Council. *International Residential Code™ for One- and Two-Family*

Dwellings. International Code Council, 2000. ISBN 1-892395-17-7.
This is structure as the code enforcement officer views it. Designed to be compatible with the three largest building code agencies in the U.S.: Building Officials and Code Administrators (BOCA), International Code Council (ICC), and the Southern Building Code Congress International (SBCCI).

(ST) Ramsey, Charles G. and Harold R. Sleeper. *Architectural Graphic Standards*, 10th Edition. John Wiley and Sons, 2000. ISBN: 0-471-34816-3.
A huge book, over 1,000 pages. Best used in the library. This and other editions of the same work contain pages of span tables, as well as other good basic wood-engineering information.

Salvadori, Mario. *Why Buildings Stand Up: The Strength of Architecture.* W.W. Norton & Co., 1980 & 1990. ISBN: 0-393-30676-3.
Fun to read. Good on beams and columns. Nice integration of structural lessons with fascinating case studies such as the Brooklyn Bridge and the Eiffel Tower.

Timber Framer's Guild. *Timber-Frame Joinery & Design Workbook.* Christian & Son, 1997. ISBN: 0-9706643-1-1.
Articles from timber-framing conferences, including good ones on structure and how trusses work. Five pages of valuable tables on the design values for visually graded timbers (five-by-fives and larger), including bending and shear-stress ratings.

Traditional Timber Framing

Benson, Tedd. *Timberframe: The Art and Craft of the Post and Beam Home.* Taunton Press, 1999. ISBN: 1-56158-281-6.
A big, beautiful picture book of wonderful traditional timber framing. Inspirational.

Chappell, Steve. *A Timber Framer's Workshop.* Fox Maple Press, 1999. Distributed by Chelsea Green. ISBN: 1-889269-00-X
Describes the tools, structural considerations, design, roof framing and all the joinery details involved in timber framing. Used as the textbook at Fox Maple School. Chapter 11, Building Math & Engineering, is enlightening. Recommended.

Elliott, Stewart and Eugenie Wallas. *The Timber Framing Book.* Housesmiths Press, 1977. ISBN: 0-918238-01-3.
Hard to find now, but excellent on the simplest of timber framing joints that you might like to incorporate into your project. Covers some of the more difficult ones, too.

Sobon, Jack A. *Build a Classic Timber-Framed House.* Storey Books, 1994. ISBN: 0-88266-841-2.
Clearly illustrated joint details. Good on characteristics and types of wood.

Sobon, Jack A. and Roger Schroeder. *Timber Frame Construction.* Storey Books, 1984. ISBN: 0-88266-365-8.
I used this one in research, but the previous entry is Sobon's definitive work.

Conventional Building and Framing

Borer, Pat and Cindy Harris. *Out of the Woods: Ecological Designs for Timber Frame Housing.* Centre For Alternative Technology Publications, 1994. Distributed in North America by New Society Publishers. ISBN: 1-898049-12-2.
This well-illustrated practical little book is about the Walter Segal method of timber framing, which consists of bolting together smaller — typically "two-by" material — in a very powerful way.

(ST) Clark, Sam. *The Real Goods Independent Builder: Designing and Building a House Your Own Way.* Chelsea Green, 1996. ISBN: 0-930031-85-7.

This comprehensive book could have been listed under Timber Framing or Structure, just as well. And Design, too, if I had that category. Recommended on many levels.

(ST) Cole, John N. and Charles Wing. *From the Ground Up*. Little, Brown and Co., 1976. ISBN:0-316-15112-2.
Charles Wing is often referred to as the "father of the modern owner-builder movement." This oldie is still a goodie, and it takes the reader through every facet of building design and construction. Wing explains structure nicely. The span tables for rough-cut lumber are hard to find anywhere else.

Connell, John. *Homing Instinct*. Warner Books, 1993. ISBN: 0-446-51607-4.
This large volume takes the reader through the entire home-building design-and-build process, written by the founder of the Yestermorrow Design/Build School. Both conventional and slightly less conventional designs are covered. Good commentary on structure in the appendices.

Fine Homebuilding. *Foundations and Concrete Work*. Taunton Press, 1998. ISBN: 1-56158-330-8.
Conventional and unconventional stuff here. The articles on site layout, the slab-on-grade foundation, and the rubble-trench foundation are the clearest I've seen, and the other 20-odd articles aren't bad, either.

Fine Homebuilding. *Framing Roofs*. Taunton Press, 1997. ISBN: 1-56158-209-3.
Contains 32 articles on roofing, including a couple of good ones on trusses, all clearly illustrated in the excellent Fine Homebuilding style.

Haun, Larry. *Homebuilding Basics: Carpentry*. Taunton Press, 1999. ISBN: 1-56158-167-4.
Excellent on carpentry, including framing floors, walls, stairs, ceilings, and roofs. Written by a long-time carpenter who knows his stuff and how to explain it. Very well illustrated.

(ST) Nash, George. *Do-It-Yourself Housebuilding*. Sterling, 1995. ISBN: 0-8069-0424-0.
This huge well-written volume is the one book you need to build a conventional house. It's all here — foundations, electric, plumbing, framing, roofing.

Roy, Rob. *The Sauna*. Chelsea Green, 1996. ISBN: 0-930031-87-3.
No, I'm not trying to push my own book here. Really. But Chapter 3 has 42 pages of detailed information about how to build the post-and-beam sauna seen in Figures 2.19, 2.20, and 2.21, including the foundation. This building would be a great little practice project, and could be used as a sauna, playhouse, guest cabin, or garden shed.

(ST) Spence, William P. *Residential Framing: A Homebuilder's Construction Guide*. Sterling, 1993. ISBN: 0-8069-8594-1.
This one is an excellent companion to the volume in your hands. Good illustrations on the use of mechanical fasteners. Strong on post, plank and beam, roof framing, and trusses. Recommended.

Infilling

Evans, Ianto, Michael G. Smith, and Linda Smiley. *The Hand-Sculpted House: A Practical and Philosophical Guide to Building a Cob Cottage*. Chelsea Green, 2002. ISBN: 1-890132-34-9.
Simply the most complete book on building with cob. The "philosophical" part is good, too.

Kennedy, Joseph F, Michael G. Smith, and Catherine Wanek. *The Art of Natural Building*. New Society Publishers, 2002. ISBN: 0-86571-433-9.
Covers all styles of natural infilling methods: cob, cordwood, light clay, rammed earth, straw bale, and more.

Magwood, Chris and Peter Mack. *Straw Bale Building: How to Plan, Design and Build with Straw*. New Society Publishers, 2000. ISBN: 0-86571-403-7.

Good practical information about building a house with straw bales, with or without a timber frame.

Morley, Michael. *Building With Structural Insulated Panels.* Taunton Press, 2000. ISBN: 1-56158-351-0. *Everything you need to know about structural insulated panels (SIPS). You can actually build a house of these panels, even the roof, without a timber frame, but they are commonly used in combination with timber framing. See also Organizations in Appendix C.*

Roy, Rob. *Complete Book of Cordwood Masonry Housebuilding: the Earthwood Method.* Sterling, 1992. ISBN: 0-8069-8590-9.

Covers cordwood masonry, the floating-slab foundation, the post-and-beam sauna, and the step-by-step construction of the Earthwood house and outbuildings. Sadly, this book went out of print in 2003. Get it through Amazon, E-bay or inter-library loan.

Roy, Rob. *Cordwood Building: The State of the Art.* New Society Publishers, 2003. ISBN: 0-86571-475-4. *Up-to-date information about cordwood masonry by over twenty of the field's leading shakers and doers.*

Index

About the Author

ROB ROY HAS BEEN TEACHING ALTERNATIVE BUILDING METHODS to owner-builders since 1978, and has become well-known as a writer and educator in fields as disparate as cordwood masonry, earth-sheltered housing, saunas, stone circles and mortgage freedom. This is his twelfth book for owner-builders. He has also created four published videos, also for owner-builders. With his wife Jaki, Rob started Earthwood Building School in 1981. The couple teaches their building techniques all over the world, but their home is at Earthwood in West Chazy, New York. Their website is <**http://www.cordwoodmasonry.com**>.

If you have enjoyed *Timber Framing for the Rest of Us* you might also enjoy other

BOOKS TO BUILD A NEW SOCIETY

Our books provide positive solutions for people who want to make a difference. We specialize in:

Sustainable Living • Ecological Design and Planning • Natural Building & Appropriate Technology
New Forestry • Environment and Justice • Conscientious Commerce • Progressive Leadership
Educational and Parenting Resources • Resistance and Community • Nonviolence

For a full list of NSP's titles, please call 1-800-567-6772 or check out our web site at:
www.newsociety.com

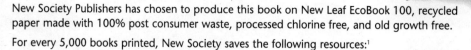

New Society Publishers

ENVIRONMENTAL BENEFITS STATEMENT

New Society Publishers has chosen to produce this book on New Leaf EcoBook 100, recycled paper made with 100% post consumer waste, processed chlorine free, and old growth free.

For every 5,000 books printed, New Society saves the following resources:[1]

33	Trees
3,011	Pounds of Solid Waste
3,313	Gallons of Water
4,321	Kilowatt Hours of Electricity
5,474	Pounds of Greenhouse Gases
24	Pounds of HAPs, VOCs, and AOX Combined
8	Cubic Yards of Landfill Space

[1]Environmental benefits are calculated based on research done by the Environmental Defense Fund and other members of the Paper Task Force who study the environmental impacts of the paper industry.

For more information on this environmental benefits statement, or to inquire about environmentally friendly papers, please contact New Leaf Paper – info@newleafpaper.com Tel: 888 • 989 • 5323.

NEW SOCIETY PUBLISHERS